Companion Guide to the

Rosh Hashanah Prayer Service

Companion Guide to the

Rosh Hashanah Prayer Service

Featuring

**EXPLANATIONS OF
SIGNIFICANT PRAYERS**

SELECTED TRANSLITERATIONS

PARABLES & ESSAYS

by Moshe I. Sorscher

Companion Guide to the

ROSH HASHANAH PRAYER SERVICE

ISBN # 1-880582-13-9
Library of Congress Catalog # 94-077883

Grateful acknowledgement is made to the following for permission to
reprint previously published material: Quoted passages from *Horeb* by
Samson Raphael Hirsch, translated by Dr. I. Grunfeld, reprinted by
permission of The Soncino Press, Ltd. Passages from the *Companion to the
Machzor* by Rabbi A.L. Rubinstein reprinted by permission of J. Lehman,
distributor. We have also adapted questions and answers from *What is the
Reason* by Rabbi Chaim Press, by permission of Rabbi Press.

THE JUDAICA PRESS, Inc.
123 Ditmas Avenue
Brooklyn, NY 11218
718-972-6200   800-972-6201

Table of Contents

Prayer Service

Essays & Parables

Dedicated to the memory of our beloved Father

Jack Glass

יעקב פינחס בן יהושע אלקנה הלוי ע"ה

A man whose most prized possession
was his Prayer Book.

May his singular devotion to prayer
serve as an inspiration to all
who make use of this Guide.

Lenny and Estelle Glass and Family
Elizabeth, New Jersey

Foreword

The Companion Guide to the Rosh Hashanah Prayer Service developed by Moshe I. Sorscher is the product of years of experience in guiding Jews who are beginning to recover their heritage in Jewish prayers and traditions. The newcomer, who is unfamiliar with the language and the ritual, initially finds the quest to be beset by mountainous difficulties. Gifted guides and devoted teachers have staked out paths and developed tools to make the summit of Jewish self-discovery available to all who seek it. Moshe Sorscher, as coordinator of the Outreach Program of Young Israel of Flatbush, has been eminently successful in his endeavors. He has encouraged and guided many who took the first faltering steps to find their way to join the Congregation in full worship services.

His goals have been reached by his ability to formulate practical and inspirational methods and texts. They enable the neophyte to progress in using and understanding the Jewish prayer book, by brief explanations and helpful transliterations.

The Companion Guide to the Rosh Hashanah Prayer Service will prove very helpful to all who have little acquaintance with the High Holiday Services, as well as to Congregations who conduct outreach programs. Its greatest commendation comes from the many whom it has elevated to appreciate the tremendous devotional experience of the High Holidays.

Rabbi Solomon J. Sharfman

(Rabbi Sharfman is the Rabbi Emeritus of Young Israel of Flatbush, having served his Congregation for over 45 years. He and his wife now reside in Israel.)

Foreword

Prayer is referred to by the Torah as "service of the heart." This phrase implies that proper prayer has two components: 1) service —a tangible aspect, and 2) the heart—feeling and concentration. It is necessary, therefore, to pray by actually pronouncing the words; mere thought will not suffice, for service must be tangible. Yet, if one only pronounces the words without understanding their meaning and significance, the heart has not been involved.

Moshe I. Sorscher has provided a very valuable service by producing *The Companion Guide to the Rosh Hashanah Prayer Service.* This labor of love is inspired by his selfless dedication to the Young Israel of Flatbush Beginner's Service, where he teaches love and devotion to prayer on a weekly basis. As he has done in his previous works, he engages both the lips and the heart. Transliterations are provided to enable those not fluent in Hebrew to participate in praying with the Congregation. The entire structure of the prayer service together with comments about individual prayers is explained in a clear, concise manner, providing enlightenment and inspiration.

May this guide serve as a vehicle for many Jews all over the country to improve their *Rosh Hashanah* praying. May it serve as a catalyst to cause Jews to draw closer to A-mighty G-d and may these bonds between man and his Creator forged on *Rosh Hashanah,* endure for the entire year.

Rabbi Kenneth Auman
Rabbi, Young Israel of Flatbush

Acknowledgments

The publication of this book came about as a result of my work in the Outreach Program of my synagogue, Young Israel of Flatbush in Brooklyn, N.Y. Our organization has dedicated itself to reaching out to help and acquaint our brethren with the magnificent heritage and traditions of the Jewish people.

The words are not easily available to express thanks and appreciation to the Young Israel for the opportunity I have been given to get involved in the noble work of *Kiruv*. Our program was fostered by the National Jewish Outreach Program and I am grateful to Rabbis Ephraim Buchwald and Yitzchak Rosenbaum for their inspiration in helping our program from its infancy. In only two short years, we have been instrumental in changing the lives of scores of individuals.

I also wish to recognize the assistance rendered by our spiritual leader, Rabbi Kenneth Auman, the Young Israel administration and the very dedicated members of our committee for their wholehearted support and co-operation.

This book is a much expanded edition of my first publication, prepared two years ago. As before, Ms. P'nina Shiller painstakingly spent many hours typesetting and editing the book, and my dear friend, Jack Goldman ה"ע, provided very valuable technical assistance. Regretfully, we all suffered an irreplaceable loss with his tragic passing. His family continues his legacy and I am extremely grateful to the editors of Judaica Press, who spent many hours editing and improving my original work.

My dear wife, Naomi, and my family deserve much credit for their continued support and patience in providing me with the atmosphere conducive to the writing of this book, for which I am truly grateful.

And, finally, my deepest and most humble thanks are reserved for the King of Kings, for the Creator of all things, who has blessed me with the opportunity and selected me as the vehicle to be involved in reaching hundreds of our Jewish brethren. May I only be worthy to merit His continued blessings.

Moshe I. Sorscher
August, 1994

Preface

This edition of *The Companion Guide to the Rosh Hashanah Prayer Service* has been prepared to help worshippers become better acquainted with the prayer service. It is intended to be a short synopsis of the focal points, order and structure of the *Rosh Hashanah* prayers.

For the benefit of worshippers whose Hebrew reading is minimal, I have included an English transliteration of selected hymns and liturgical passages. For the transliteration, I used the *Sephardic* pronunciation since that is what is commonly used in spoken Modern Hebrew.

In addition I have elaborated on important prayers in the *machzor* and on *Rosh Hashanah* themes and customs. A few inspirational parables have also been included plus description and background on synagogue procedures.

This companion guide is to be used together with a High Holiday prayer book. In order to make this guide accessible to as many people as possible, I have indicated the corresponding pages in the *Artscroll Machzor, Metsudah Machzor, Birnbaum Machzor* (both the combined edition and the 2-volume edition) and the *Lubavitch Machzor* (i.e., *nusach* ARI). The page numbers are preceded by the letters: **A** for *Artscroll*, **B** for *Birnbaum*, **BC** for *Birnbaum* Combined (i.e., the one volume edition of *Rosh Hashanah* and *Yom Kippur*), **M** for *Metsudah* and **L** for *Lubavitch*.

I have transliterated many of the most important and well known prayers and hymns. Unfortunately, the need for brevity has not permitted me to transliterate those that were overly lengthy. In many of the liturgical poems only the initial four stanzas have been transliterated, as usually only these are sung together by the *Chazan* or Congregation. In addition, in certain parts of the prayer service, where prayers are said silently we have skipped pages in the *machzor.*

Feel free to use the guide in any way best suited for you. You may find it useful to have both the *machzor* and the guide opened at the appropriate place and to glance back and forth from one to the other, or to refer to the guidebook only for the transliterations or the explanations of the prayers. Beginning Hebrew readers will find the transliterations very helpful as a phonetic guide.

All of the above was designed to help readers gain a better understanding of the *Rosh Hashanah* services so that the prayers could be appreciated more deeply.

Finally, one approaches the holiday with awe, with a sense of holiness and with confidence that we will be blessed with a happy and healthy year.

Moshe I. Sorscher

Introduction

For Jews, the beginning of the New Year is not a time for excessive celebration or overindulgence. It is a time for meditation, reflection and sincere repentance. Having purified ourselves of our failings of the past year, we can go forward in the New Year spiritually refreshed, with our souls uplifted and reinvigorated.

The great 19th century scholar, Samson Raphael Hirsch wrote that our duty on *Rosh Hashanah* is to acknowledge anew our relationship with G-d. *Rosh Hashanah* calls us from our worldly concerns and our day-to-day work to renew ourselves and truly examine G-d's presence in our life. As a result of this introspection we hope to rise to a purer life.

The Birthday of the Universe

According to the Talmud, the world was created on *Rosh Hashanah.* One of the prayers of the *Rosh Hashanah* service describes this fact:

"Today is the birthday of the world. On this day all creatures of the world stand in judgment—either as G-d's children or as servants. If as children, be merciful with us as a father has mercy for [his] children. If as servants, our eyes are turned to You, until You will be gracious to us and release our verdict as the light, O Awesome and Holy One."

But *Rosh Hashanah* which literally means—"head of the year" is a celebration not only of the universe's creation but also of our own creation. With *Rosh Hashanah* we have the opportunity to recreate ourselves. After serious self-examination we can repent of past deeds and begin again.

The Jewish month in which *Rosh Hashanah* falls is *Tishray*, which also marks the birth of many of our ancestors. The first man, Adam was created in *Tishray* and, according to Rabbi Eliezer (*Rosh Hashanah* 10b, 11a) the patriarch Abraham was born in *Tishray*. It is fitting that Abraham was born in *Tishray*, for he was the beginning of a new world of monotheism. Rabbi Eliezer notes that the patriarch Jacob was also born in *Tishray*.

Rosh Hashanah, in addition, was a fertile month for our matriarchs—Sarah, childless until age ninety, was finally given the gift of a child in *Tishray*—as was Rachel. Hannah, too, barren for many years finally conceived the prophet Samuel in *Tishray*.

Other important events in Jewish history occurred on *Rosh Hashanah:* Joseph was freed from an Egyptian prison and went on to become viceroy of Egypt. And this same day marked the beginning of the redemption of our enslaved ancestors in Egypt. And in Jerusalem the first Temple was also dedicated in *Tishray*.

A Day of Divine Judgment

Rosh Hashanah is sometimes called *Yom Hadin* which in Hebrew means "Day of Judgment," signifying that we will be judged on this day according to our actions. It is also the day when we must review our deeds of the past year. This aspect is dwelt on in many of *Rosh Hashanah's* prayers and hymns.

The *Midrash* (*Leviticus Rabbah* 29:1) states that on the very first *Rosh Hashanah* Adam committed his sin of disobeying G-d. G-d judged him, forgave him and as a sign to his children, G-d said: "Just as you were judged before me on this day and emerged forgiven, so will your children be judged this day and will be forgiven." It is for this reason that G-d sees fit to judge mankind every year on this day.

G-d in his kindness toward us, remembers us and reviews our deeds on *Rosh Hashanah* (*Sefer Hachinuch, Mitzvah* 311). G-d gives us the chance to atone so that our sins will not accumulate. When our good and bad deeds are evenly balanced, He tips the scales of justice and He pardons us. If there are misdeeds requiring cleansing, He exacts payment for them little by little. This Holy Day ensures the survival of the world, and it is fitting that *Rosh Hashanah* is celebrated as a festival. Since it is also the time when everyone is judged, it is proper to observe the day with greater reverence than all other festival days of the year.

Shofar

Rosh Hashanah is also called *Yom Teruah* which means "Day of sounding the ram's horn," which is one of the Biblical names for *Rosh Hashanah.* The *shofar* ("ram's horn") is sounded to arouse those who have fallen asleep in life, remind them of the Law of Truth revealed at Sinai and announce the sure advent of the Redemption.

It is obligatory to hear the *shofar* on *Rosh Hashanah.* It stirs us to explore our lives and improve our ways. "After the *shofar* has been sounded a new, more sublime light descends, so sublime a light as has never shone since the world began" *(Tanya Iggeret Hakodesh).*

The *shofar* is the oldest surviving type of wind instrument. Although usually a ram's horn is used to make a *shofar,* the horn of any kosher animal can be used, except that of an ox or bull, which recall the sin of the golden calf.

On each of the two days of *Rosh Hashanah,* the *shofar* is blown 100 times as a call for repentance. Three distinct sounds are used: *tekiah,* a long unbroken sound; *shevarim,* a three-part plaintive sound; and *teruah,* a nine-part broken sound (three *shevarim*).

When the Temple still stood, the *shofar* was actually sounded frequently—when kings were anointed, when peace treaties were signed, over sacrifices, to signal the end of the workday and to welcome the Sabbath and the new moon.

The Scriptural basis for the blowing of the *shofar* comes from *Leviticus* 23:24, when G-d told Moses, "Speak unto the children of Israel, saying: In the seventh month [*Tishray*], in the first day of the month, shall be a solemn rest unto you, a memorial proclaimed with the blast of horns, a holy convocation." Numbers 29:1 says "[the first of *Tishray*] is a day of blowing the horn unto you."

When our fate has been sealed, at the conclusion of the *N'eelah* service of *Yom Kippur*, the *shofar* is sounded one last time. The sound heralds the departure of the *Shechinah* ("Divine Presence") and arouses within us the hope of the coming of the Messiah. We also hope that G-d has accepted our prayers and penitence and has forgiven our sins.

Tashlich

To symbolize the casting away of our sins, we go to the shore of a river or other body of water to recite special prayers (which include Psalms and the last verses from the Book of *Micah*, "You shall cast all their sins into the depths of the sea."). This is done on the first day of *Rosh Hashanah*, except when this day is *Shabbat*. If the *Tashlich* prayer cannot be recited at this time, it may be said at any time during the Penitential period.

The word *Tashlich* means "to cast away," which alludes to G-d casting away the transgressions of Israel. It is customary to put crumbs of bread into one's pockets and then shake them out while reciting the prayer, to symbolize our wish to get rid of our sins and be forgiven by G-d.

The *Midrash* relates that as Abraham traveled to Mount Moriah to sacrifice his son Isaac, he found his path blocked by a body of water. Abraham fearlessly entered the water and when it rose to his shoulders, he cried to G-d for help. The waters receded. With *Taschlich* we commemorate Abraham's absolute commitment to G-d's will. This incident took place on *Rosh Hashanah*.

It is preferable to recite *Tashlich* at a body of water containing fish, to remind us that just as fish are protected by the water in which they live, we pray that we too will be protected by G-d. In addition, just as a fish swimming freely can suddenly be caught by a net, so can we just as helplessly and just as suddenly fall into sin. And even as the eyes of fish are always open, so do we pray that G-d too keep watch on His people.

Symbolic foods

So conscious are we that we will be judged on *Rosh Hashanah* and that our fate hangs by a thread that even the foods we eat on *Rosh Hashanah* are carefully chosen. It is customary on *Rosh Hashanah* to eat foods that are omens for the coming year. In general sweet foods are eaten for they signal our wish for a sweet year. The types of foods vary depending on each family's country of origin.

On *Rosh Hashanah* pomegranates grace the table of many Jews throughout the world. Since a pomegranate always has an abundance of seeds, so too do we wish that our merits and good deeds will be judged as numerous as the seeds in a pomegranate. The pomegranate has been compared in the *Talmud* to a sinner, since just like even the poorest sample of pomegranate is abundant with seed so must a few good deeds be found in even the worst sinner (*Sanhedrin* 37a).

Carrot *tzimmes* is also typical *Rosh Hashanah* fare and that is because besides being a sweet dish, the Yiddish word for carrot is *merren,* the same word for multiply or many. We pray that our merits be considered many. The beet is another vegetable that is eaten on *Rosh Hashanah*. In Aramaic (once spoken quite widely by Jews and the language of the Babylonian *Talmud*) the word for beet is *silka,* also the word for remove. By eating this food we pray that our sins will be removed. Dates are eaten because the Aramaic word for date is *tamra,* similar to the Aramaic word for end. This signifies our hope that the power of our enemies will come to an end.

Fish is often on the *Rosh Hashanah* menu as an appetizer. This is because fish are prolific, reproducing rapidly and abundantly. We too wish to be fertile—both individually and as a people. The head of a fish is the choice portion because we hope to be the heads of our communities in all our endeavors and particularly in our righteousness (*Shulchan Aruch* 583:2). Another choice fish is *gefilte* fish as the word *gefilte* in Yiddish means filled. We prayer that our pleas to G-d will be answered and fulfilled.

Another very old custom is to eat ram (mutton) to remind us of the ram that Abraham sacrificed instead of his son.

It is also customary to eat a new fruit of the season or a fruit that has not been eaten all year. We do this on the second night of *Rosh Hashanah* so that we can say the *Shehecheyanu* blessing, thanking G-d for allowing us to reach this year so that we are able to continue keeping His commandments. Some popular choices include fresh figs, papayas and mangos. The *Shehecheyanu* blessing can also be said on new clothing that has been bought to be worn on *Rosh Hashanah.*

Generally vinegary, sour, bitter and spicy foods are avoided. Nuts are not eaten because the Hebrew for nut has the same numerical value as the Hebrew word for sin.

In many Jewish communities the *challah* (loaf of bread) is shaped in the form of a ladder. This reminds us of Jacob's dream in which heaven and earth were connected—this symbolizes our wish that our prayers flow upwards with ease. The ladder also symbolizes man's fate—G-d will either raise us or lower us—we will either succeed or fail, our future can go either way.

It is customary to dip the *challah* into honey or sugar so as to remind ourselves to pray for a sweet year. In *Psalms* (as well as other places) we find that honey is symbolic of plenty, "Then He would feed them with the fat of wheat and I would sate you with honey from a rock." (81:17) This psalm was also sung when *Rosh Hashanah* sacrifices were offered in the Temple. In addition, the numerical value for the Hebrew word for honey, *devash* is the same as for *Av Ha-rahamim,* "O Father of Mercy," which again symbolizes our prayer that G-d have mercy on us. Thus honey is eaten in other forms. Honey cake, also known as *lekach,* is a typical

Rosh Hashanah desert. The *challah* for *Rosh Hashanah* is also traditionally sweetened either with honey or with raisins.

Another tradition is to dip an apple into honey. Why an apple? Sages say that on most fruit trees the leaves appear before the fruit and provide protection for the delicate young fruit. The apple, however, bursts forth before the leaves. The people of Israel are likened to an apple because we are willing to lead Jewish lives even when our lives are at risk.

Good Omens

In many Jewish communities there is much cleaning and organizing in the house before *Rosh Hashanah*. This symbolizes our wish for an authentic new beginning. New clothes are also bought for *Rosh Hashanah* not only because it is a special day but also to express how confident we feel that we will be judged favorably by G-d. In the same vein it is customary to get a haircut.

The *Machzor*

The prayer book for festivals is called a *machzor*, which in Hebrew means "cycle," suggesting the yearly cycle of festival prayers. The *machzor* consists of selections and readings from the *Torah* and the *Talmud* that were put together by Divinely inspired prophets and sages.

The Ten Days of Repentance

In the Talmud it says: It is written in *Isaiah* "Seek the Lord while He may be found." When can an individual find G-d? Rabbah b. Abbuha said: These are the ten days between New Year and the Day of Atonement" (*Rosh. Hashanah* 18a).

Rosh Hashanah inaugurates a ten-day period known as *Aseret Y'may Teshuvah* ("the ten days of repentance"), culminating with the awesome day of *Yom Kippur*. On *Rosh Hashanah* our fate is inscribed and on *Yom Kippur* it is sealed. The *Talmud* states (*Rosh Hashanah* 16b) that Rabbi Kruspedai said in the name of Rabbi Yochanan: "Three books are opened [in Heaven] on *Rosh Hashanah*—one for the thoroughly wicked, one for the thoroughly righteous, and one for the intermediate. The wholly righteous are at once inscribed and sealed in the Book of Life; the wholly wicked are at once sealed and inscribed in the Book of Death; the fate of the intermediate is held suspended from *Rosh Hashanah* until *Yom Kippur*. If they are found worthy, they are inscribed for life. If they are found unworthy, they are inscribed for death." Thus we can clearly see the importance of these ten days.

May we all be granted inscription in the Book of Life and may we merit a favorable judgment by the Heavenly court. If we will heed the message of *Rosh Hashanah*, listen fervently to the sound and the meaning of the *shofar* and sincerely enter upon the road of *Teshuvah* ("repentance"), we can be assured that our prayers will be answered and we will be blessed with a happy and healthy year.

🕊 *The Language of Prayer* 🕊

rayer in any language is of course acceptable to G-d. In a congregational setting, however, Hebrew, the *lashon hakodesh*—(holy tongue) is the preferred medium. The reasons are varied. The Bible, Prophets, writings, *Mishna*, and virtually all later Rabbinic commentaries were written in Hebrew. Hebrew continues the bond with the Jewish people which began thousands of years ago. Hebrew is also the method of prayer used in synagogues throughout the world, enabling a Jew to communicate with G-d wherever he may be, just as G-d has communicated with His people wherever they are. In addition the prayer book was organized throughought many years in Hebrew. A translation simply does not convey the same nuances.

Nevertheless, one is permitted to pray in any language they understand. An old Hasidic tale illustrates the spirit of this Rabbinic ruling. A young lad accompanied his father to the big city on market day. The boy, from a rural village, went with his father to the local synagogue and was moved by the intensity and devotion of the congregation immersed in prayer. Not knowing Hebrew, but having been taught the Hebrew alphabet by his father, he began to recite the Hebrew alphabet over and over again. He said "O Lord, you know what I wish to say. Here are the letters—please put them together so they make the right words."

No better prayer was offered than the pure letters that came from the heart of this little soul. Think about that as you use this book on *Rosh Hashanah*. Let every word uttered throughout your prayers be said thoughtfully and with an attentive spirit. This is the essence of prayer. As you use this book, have these thoughts in mind and your prayers, if recited with devotion, will surely reach the heavenly throne.

Rabbi Nachman of Breslov, the great 18th century Hasidic Rebbe said that every word of a prayer is like a rose that one has picked from a bush. One continues to pray until a bouquet of blessings has been formed, until one has completed a beautiful wreath of glory for G-d.

Outline of
Rosh Hashanah Services

The *Rosh Hashanah* Services consist of several major prayers. The components of these prayer are outlined below. The prayers for both days of *Rosh Hashanah* are essentially the same.

Maariv—The Evening Service
Maariv — The Evening Prayer
Barchu — Blessing G-d
The *Shema* — Declaration of Faith
Shemoneh Esray — *The Amida,* The Silent Devotion
Concluding hymns

Shacharit—The Morning Service
Birchot Hashachar — Morning Blessings
Pesukay D'zimrah — Psalms of Praise
The *Shema* and its blessings — Declaration of Faith
Shemoneh Esray — *The Amida,* The Silent Devotion
Chazan's repetition of *Shemoneh Esray*
  Piyutim — Liturgical hymns
  Kedushah — Sanctification of G-d's Name

Kriyat Hatorah—The *Torah* Service
Removal of the *Torahs* from the *Aron*
The *Torah* Reading
The Additional *Torah* Reading
The *Haftarah* — Reading from the Prophets
Tkiyat Shofar — The Sounding of the *Shofar*
Returning the *Torahs* to the *Aron*

Mussaf — The Additional Service

Chazan's Prayer
Shemoneh Esray — *The Amida,* The Silent Devotion
Chazan's Repetition of the *Shemoneh Esray*
   Unetaneh Tokef — Let us declare
   Kedushah — Sanctification of G-d's Name
   Additional Soundings of the *shofar*
   Birkat Kohanim — Blessing of the Priests

Mincha — The Afternoon Service

Shemoneh Esray — *The Amida,* The Silent Devotion
Chazan's Repetition of the *Shemoneh Esray*
Kedushah — Sanctification of G-d's Name

Maariv — The Evening Service

Shemoneh Esray — *The Amida,* The Silent Devotion
Havdalah — Parting ceremony (recited at the close of the final day of *Rosh Hashanah*).

How To Use This Guide

The *Rosh Hashanah* Companion Guide is to be used together with a High Holiday prayer book. In order to make this guide accessible to as many people as possible, we have indicated the corresponding pages in the *Artscroll Machzor (Ashkenaz), Metsudah Machzor, Birnbaum Machzor (Ashkenaz*—both the combined edition and the 2-volume edition) and the *Lubavitch Machzor* (i.e., *nusach Ha-Ari*).

The page numbers are preceded by the letters:

A for *Artscroll,*

B for *Birnbaum,*

BC for *Birnbaum* combined (i.e., the one volume edition of *Rosh Hashanah* and *Yom Kippur*),

M for *Metsudah* and

L for *Lubavitch.*

1

Mincha - Maariv
Afternoon - Evening Services

A 20 BC 3 B 3 M 8 L 14

Mincha—The *Rosh Hashanah* Afternoon Service is the same as the weekday Afternoon Service. It consists of a beautiful introductory Psalm, *Ashray* ("Fortunate"), followed by the *Shemoneh Esray* (Silent Devotion) and concludes with *Alaynu* (Declaration of Faith).

However, whenever *Mincha* is said in the synagogue there are a few additions. Before reciting the Silent Devotion, the *Chazan* chants the *Half Kaddish,* and when everyone is finished with the Silent Devotion the *Chazan* will repeat it, inserting the *Kedushah* (Sanctification) into the repetition. This is the most important part of the prayer service as the Congregation rises and in unison recites praise to G-d. The Congregation should follow the balance of the repetition, answering *Amen* where applicable.

After the repetition of the *Shemoneh Esray*, the *Full Kaddish* is recited by the *Chazan* which is followed by *Alaynu*. If there are mourners in the synagogue, the *Mourner's Kaddish* follows *(please see page 14)*.

The *Mincha* Service is the final prayer of the prior year, hence added concentration and devotion are obligatory. As such, as we enter the New Year we seek the blessings of G-d for good health and peace. We also want to be judged favorably by the Almighty, so our attitude at this time is somber, yet filled with hopeful anticipation as we begin the Ten-Day Penitential period, culminating with the Day of Atonement.

When Rosh Hashanah *falls on the Sabbath, the Psalms and Hymns which normally would be chanted at the Friday Evening Service are not recited.* Kabbalat Shabbat *("Acceptance of the Sabbath") consists of the recital of Psalms 92 and 93.*

ᔑ MAARIV ᔑ
(Evening Service)

A 50 BC 23 B 23 M 29 L 26

The *Chazan* begins the Evening Service with *Barchu*, ("Bless"), in a melody especially reserved for the Days of Awe. In many synagogues, the Congregation chants the melody together with the *Chazan*.

ᔑ BARCHU ᔑ
("Invitation to Congregation to bless G-d")

A 50 BC 23 B 23 M 29 L 26

Barchu is the *Chazan*'s summons to the Congregation to bless G-d prior to the recitation of *Shema*. The *Chazan*'s call to us and our response acknowledge that we realize that G-d is the source of all blessings. Like certain other parts of the prayer service (e.g., *Kaddish*, *Kedushah*, the *Torah* Reading), the recital of *Barchu* requires a *minyan* (a quorum of at least ten adult males).

The Chazan *and Congregation bow slightly at the command* Barchu, *and everyone stands erect when G-d's name is recited.*

Chazan **Barchu Et Adonai Ham-vorach**
("Bless G-d, the Blessed One")

Everyone again bows at the word Baruch *and straightens up at G-d's name.*

Cong. **Baruch Adonai Ham-vorach L'olam Va-ed**

("Blessed is G-d, the Blessed One for all of eternity")

This sentence is repeated by the Chazan.

℘ THE BLESSINGS PRECEDING THE SHEMA ℘

A 50   BC 23   B 23   M 29   L 26

Following *Barchu*, two blessings precede the *Shema*. The first blessing, *Asher Bidvaro* ("Who, by His word"), describes G-d's control over nature and praises Him as the Creator of the heavenly bodies and for His power to create night and day. This blessing concludes with the words *Hama-ariv Aravim* ("Who brings on evenings").

The second blessing, *Ahavat Olam* ("Eternal love"), said just prior to reciting the *Shema*, describes G-d's love for His people and praises Him for giving us the *Torah* to study and obey, for it is the essence of our lives. This blessing concludes with the words *Ohayv Amo Yisrael* ("Who loves His nation Israel").

℘ THE SHEMA ℘

(Acceptance of G-d's Sovereignty)

The passage from Deuteronomy (6:4), "Hear O Israel, The Lord is our G-d, The Lord is One," and the three paragraphs that follow are part of both the daily morning and evening prayers. The *Shema* is the single most important sentence in the liturgy. It is not a prayer but rather an affirmation of the oneness of G-d.

The first paragraph of the *Shema* describes how we should love G-d with all our heart, with all our soul and with all our might, and in it we are commanded to convey this love to the next generation. This section also contains the two *mitzvot* ("commandments") of *tefillin* and *mezuzah*.

In the second paragraph we are commanded as a Jewish nation to accept G-d's commandments, and promised reward if we fulfill them, punishment if we do not. Again we are enjoined to teach these commandments to our children and

✍ *Understanding Shema* ✒

he *Shema* is the Jew's confession of faith and proclamation of the absolute oneness and uniqueness of G-d. It is often the first religious sentence a Jewish child is taught.

In Deuteronomy (6:6-7) we are told to recite the Shema twice daily: "These words that I command you today shall be upon your heart, and you shall impress them sharply upon your sons and speak of them when you sit in your house and when you walk upon the way, when you lie down and when you get up."

We are told in the *Talmud* (*Berakhot* 4b) that the *Shema* should be recited in bed every night before going to sleep. The *Shema* is also said by relatives and friends on behalf of a dying Jew. And it is the last sentence to be uttered by Jews on their deathbed.

Unknown numbers of Jewish martyrs met their death with the words of the *Shema* on their lips. In the 2nd century C.E. Rabbi Akiva recited the first portion of the *Shema* while being tortured to death by the Romans for publicly teaching Torah. He said that he welcomed his sufferings and willingly gave up his life as a way to fulfill the commandment to "love the Lord Thy G-d with all thy heart and with all thy soul". As his flesh was being torn from his body with iron combs, Rabbi Akiva recited the *Shema* with a smile. His disciples said, "Our teacher, even to this point you are happy to recite the *Shema*?" Rabbi Akiva replied, "All my life I have been troubled by the verse 'with all thy soul.' I said to myself, 'When will I have the opportunity of fulfilling it?' Now that I have the opportunity shall I not fulfill it with joy?" And so he prolonged the word *echad* until he slipped out of consciousness, and died while saying it.

The *Shema* is so important and so well summarizes the basic principles of Judaism that its first two paragraphs are inscribed on the parchment scrolls of both the *mezuzah* and *tefillin*.

to observe the *mitzvot* of *tefillin* and *mezuzah*.

The third paragraph details the laws of *tzitzit* ("fringes"), which serve to remind us of the *Torah*'s precepts and recalls our exodus from Egypt.

So important is the *Shema* that it must be recited with undivided attention. To concentrate, the congregants cover their eyes while reciting the first verse. The recitation of the *Shema* represents the acceptance of G-d's absolute sovereignty.

SHEMA YISRAEL

A 52 BC 23 B 23 M 31 L 27

Chazan and Cong. recite aloud, carefully enunciating each word.

Shema Yisrael, Adonai Elohaynu, Adonai Echad

("Hear O Israel, The Lord is our G-d, The Lord is One")

Chazan and Cong. recite quietly.

Baruch Shem K'vod Malchuto L'olam Va-ed

("Blessed be the name of the glory of His Kingdom forever and ever")

V'AHAVTA

("And you shall love")

Cong. recites softly to themselves.

**V'ahavta et Adonai Elohecha, b'chol l'vav'cha,
uv'chol nafsh'cha, uv'chol m'odecha. V'hayu
had'varim ha-eleh, asher Anochee m'tzav'cha
hayom, al l'vavecha. V'sheenantam l'vanecha,
v'deebarta bam, b'shivt'cha b'vaytecha, uv'lecht'cha
vaderech, uv'shochb'cha uv'kumecha.
Uk'shartam l'ot al yadecha, v'hayu l'totafot bayn
aynecha. Uch'tavtam al m'zuzot baytecha, uvish'arecha.**

V'HAYA

("And it will come to pass")

Cong. recites softly to themselves.

**V'haya im sha-moah tishm'u el mitzvotai, asher
Anochee m'tzaveh et-chem hayom, l'ahavah et Adonai**

Elohaychem ul'avdo, b'chol l'vavchem uv'chol
nafsh'chem. V'natati m'tar artz'chem b'eeto, yoreh
umalkosh, v'asafta d'ganecha, v'teerosh'cha
v'yitz-harecha. V'natati aysev b'sadcha livhemtecha,
v'achalta v'savata. Heeshamru lachem, pen yifteh
l'vavchem, v'sartem va-avad'tem elohim achayrim,
v'hishtachaveetem lahem. V'chara af Adonai bachem,
v'atzar et hashamayim, v'lo yihyeh matar,
v'ha-adamah lo teetayn et y'vulah, va-avadtem m'hayrah,
may-al ha-aretz hatovah, asher Adonai notayn lachem.
V'samtem et d'varai ayleh al l'vavchem v'al nafsh'chem,
uk'shartem otam l'ot al yedchem, v'hayu l'totafot
bayn aynaychem. V'leemadtem otam et b'naychem,
l'dabayr bam, b'shivt'cha b'vaytecha,
uv'lecht'cha vaderech, uv'shochb'cha uv'kumecha.
Uch'tavtam al m'zuzot baytecha, uvish'arecha.
L'ma-an yirbu y'maychem, veeymay v'naychem
al ha-adamah asher nishba Adonai la-avotaychem
latayt lahem, keeymay hashamayim al ha-aretz.

VAYOMER
("And G-d said")

Cong. recites softly to themselves.

Vayomer Adonai el Moshe laymor. Dabayr el B'nay
Yisrael, v'amarta alayhem, v'asu lahem Tzitzit,
al kanfay vigdayhem l'dorotam, v'natnu al Tzitzit
hakanaf p'til t'chaylet. V'haya lachem L'Tzitzit,
ur'eetem oto, uz'chartem et kol mitzvot Adonai,
va-aseetem otam. V'lo taturu acharay l'vavchem,
v'acharay aynaychem asher atem zonim acharayhem.
L'ma-an tizk'ru, va-aseetem et kol mitzvotai, v'heyeetem
k'doshim laylohaychem. Ani Adonai Elohaychem,
asher hotzaytee etchem may-eretz Mitzrayim, lihyot
lachem laylohim, Ani

Make sure these final three words are said without interruption:

Adonai Elohaychem, emet.

𝒯 CONCLUDING BLESSINGS FOLLOWING THE SHEMA 𝒯

Two blessings follow the *Shema*. The first refers to the exodus of the Children of Israel from Egypt and the second describes the protection that G-d provides us with under His *Succah* ("tabernacle") of peace. In the middle of the recitation of the first blessing, Congregations usually sing the following praise of G-d:

MI CHAMOCHAH
("Who is like You")

A 58   BC 27   B 27   M 37   L 29

Cong. recites, Chazan *repeats, or sung in unison.*

**Mi chamochah ba-aylim Adonai,
mi kamochah ne-edar bakodesh,
norah t'hilot o-seh feleh.**

ADONAI YIMLOCH
("G-d will reign[for all eternity]")

A 58   BC 27   B 27   M 37   L 29

Cong. recites, Chazan *repeats, or sung in unison.*

Adonai Yimloch L'olam Va-ed.

[When Rosh Hashanah *falls on the Sabbath, the Congregation chants the following Biblical verses (Exodus 31:16-17) referring to the Sabbath, which the* Chazan *repeats:]*

V'SHAMRU
("And they shall preserve")

A 60   BC 29   B 29   M 38   L 29

Cong. recites, Chazan *repeats.*

**V'shamru v'nay Yisrael et hashabbat,
la-asot et hashabbat l'dorotam b'rit olam.
Baynee uvayn B'nay Yisrael ot hih l'olam,
ki shayshet yamim asah Adonai et hashamayim
v'et ha-aretz, uvayom hash'vee-ee shavat va-yinafash.**

TIK'OO VACHODESH SHOFAR

("Sound the *shofar* on the New Moon")

Prior to the *Amida*, the Congregation and *Chazan* sing the passage (*Psalms* 81:4-5) that refers to *Rosh Hashanah*.

Tik'oo vachodesh shofar, bakeseh l'yom cha-gaynu, ki chok l'Yisrael hu, mishpat laylohay Yaakov.

("Sound the *shofar* on the New Moon, on the appointed time for the day of our festival. For it is a statute for Israel, the judgment of the G-d of Jacob")

✍ HALF KADDISH ✒

The Half *Kaddish*, written in Aramaic, was composed while the Jews were exiled in Babylonia. Its central idea is the revelation of G-d's kingship. In it we petition for G-d's kingdom to be established speedily. One of four different types of *Kaddish*, it connects various parts of the service together. Here, it introduces the *Shemoneh Esray*. The most important part of the *Kaddish* is the congregational response affirming G-d's name: *Amen, Y'hay sh'may rabbah m'varach* ... ("May His great name be blessed forever and ever").

> **A 60   BC 29   B 29   M 39   L 30**

Chazan *recites*

Yitgadal, v'yitkadash, sh'may rabbah. *Cong. responds* Amen.
B'almah di-v'ra chirutay, v'yamlich malchutay, b'chayaychon uv'yomaychon, u'v'chayay d'chol bayt Yisrael, ba-agalah uvizman kareev, v'imru, Amen. *Cong. responds* Amen.

Chazan *and Cong. recite together:* **Y'hay sh'may rabbah m'varach, l'alam ul'almay almayah.**

Yitbarach, v'yishtabach, v'yit-pa-ar, v'yit-romam, v'yit-naseh, v'yit-hadar, v'yit-aleh, v'yit-halal, sh'may d'kudshah, B'rich Hu. *Cong. responds* B'rich Hu.

L'aylah, l'aylah, mikol birchatah v'shiratah, tushb'chatah, v'ne-chematah, da-amiran b'almah, v'imru, Amen. *Cong. responds* Amen.

ᔥ SHEMONEH ESRAY ᔤ
(Silent Devotion)

| A 62 | BC 31 | B 31 | M 40 | L 30 |

The *Amida* or *Shemoneh Esray* is the central part of the Evening Service. *Amida,* another name for this prayer, is the Hebrew word for "standing," after the position one must take while saying it. *Shemoneh Esray* means "eighteen," which is the number of blessings originally included in the Silent Devotion of the weekday service. The name *Shemoneh Esray* has been retained as the name for all the silent devotional prayers, even though on the Sabbath and holidays the Silent Devotion contains only seven blessings.

The *Shemoneh Esray* is the only prayer recited at every single daily and holiday synagogue service throughout the year. The prayer is divided into three sections: Praise, Petition and Thanksgiving. The blessings of praise and thanksgiving are the same every day of the year, but on the Sabbath and Holidays, the weekday benedictions of petition are reduced from thirteen to one because on these special days, our personal needs are provided for and thus there is no need for more petitions.

The following is a summary of the three sections of the *Shemoneh Esray*:

Praise—The first of the three blessings recognizes the glory of G-d. We approach G-d as children of Abraham, Isaac and Jacob, with whom He made an eternal covenant. We come to G-d, who is kind, supports the fallen, heals the sick and eventually restores life to the dead. G-d is holy and we, His children, recognize His omniscience.

Petition—The middle blessing expresses the sanctity of the day. This section contains several paragraphs describing G-d's Kingdom and His Holiness, with prayers for the restoration of Jerusalem and the sanctity of both Israel and *Rosh Hashanah.*

Thanksgiving—Having concluded our requests, we can now close the *Amida* with three blessings expressing our gratitude. This is similar to a petitioner withdrawing from a king's royal presence. This section includes a prayer for peace as well as a request for G-d's protection.

☞ FOLLOWING THE SHEMONEH ESRAY ☜

When *Rosh Hashanah* falls on the Sabbath, special prayers honoring the Sabbath are added here. Included is the Biblical narrative of the conclusion of creation on the seventh day (Gen. 2:1-3), the seven-faceted blessing, *Magayn Avot* ("Shield of our Forefathers") and a plea that G-d sanctify the Sabbath for us and future generations as an eternal day of rest.

L'DAVID MIZMOR
("A Psalm of David")

```
A 78   BC 91   B 91   M 56   L 35
```

Biblical commentators note that King David composed this psalm to express his happiness after purchasing the land for the First Temple. Psalm 24 highlights G-d as the King of the Universe and promises the blessings of G-d to those who serve Him. It is recited by the *Chazan* and each verse is repeated by the Congregation.

☞ KADDISH SHALAYM ☜
("Full *Kaddish*")

Kaddish is the final part of every service. We praise G-d's name and reiterate our prayer that our service will be accepted. In the Evening Service of *Rosh Hashanah*, the *Kaddish Shalaym* is recited by the *Chazan* prior to the concluding hymns. The Congregation should answer the appropriate responses with great concentration, particularly the phrase, *Amen, Y'hay sh'may rabbah m'varach* . . . ("May his great name be blessed forever and ever").

A 80   BC 41   B 41   M 58   L 36

Chazan *recites.*

Yitgadal, v'yitkadash, sh'may rabbah. *Cong. responds* Amen.

B'almah di-v'ra chirutay, v'yamlich malchutay, b'chayaychon uv'yomaychon, u'v'chayay d'chol bayt Yisrael, ba-agalah uvizman kareev, v'imru, Amen. *Cong. responds* Amen.

Chazan *and Cong. recite together:* **Y'hay sh'may rabbah m'varach, l'alam ul'almay almayah.**

Yitbarach, v'yishtabach, v'yit-pa-ar, v'yit-romam, v'yit-naseh, v'yit-hadar, v'yit-aleh, v'yit-halal, sh'may d'kudshah, B'rich Hu. *Cong. responds* B'rich Hu.

L'aylah, l'aylah, mikol birchatah v'shiratah, tush-b'chatah, v'ne-chematah, da-amiran b'almah, v'imru, Amen. *Cong. responds* Amen.

Titkabel tz'lot-hon u-va-ut-hon d'chol bayt Yisrael, kadam avu-hon di vish-maya, v'imru, Amen. *Cong. responds* Amen.

Y'hay sh'lama rabbah min sh'maya, v'chayim, alaynu v'al kol Yisrael, v'imru, Amen. *Cong. responds* Amen.

Oseh hashalom bimro-mav, Hu ya-aseh shalom, alaynu v'al kol Yisrael, v'imru, Amen. *Cong. responds* Amen.

KIDDUSH
("Sanctification")

The *Chazan* recites the *Kiddush* over a cup of wine in the traditional holiday melody. The purpose of the *Kiddush* in the synagogue, originally, was to publicly sanctify the Sabbath or Holiday for the benefit of those individuals who did not have a place to eat and hence would partake of their meal in the synagogue. The custom was retained in most Congregations; however, *Kiddush* should still be recited in one's home prior to the Holiday meal.

| A 82 BC 47 B 47 M 67 L 39 |

At home, when Rosh Hashanah *falls on the Sabbath,*
begin with Vay'hee erev....

(Recite softly.) **Vay'hee erev, vay'hee voker . . .**

**Yom hashee-shee. Vay'chulu hashamayim
v'ha-aretz v'chal tz'va-am. Vay'chal Elohim bayom
hash'vee-ee m'lachto asher asah, vayish-bot bayom
hash'vee-ee mikal m'lachto asher asah.
Vay'varech Elohim et yomhash'vee-ee vay'ka-daysh
oto, ki vo shavat mikol m'lachto,
asher barah Elohim la-asot.**

Begin here on weekdays.
**Savree maranan v'rabanan v'rabotai.
Baruch atah Adonai, Elohaynu melech ha-olam,
boray p'ri hagafen.** *Listeners respond* Amen.

When Rosh Hashanah *falls on the Sabbath,*
insert the words in parentheses.

**Baruch atah Adonai, Elohaynu melech ha-olam,
asher bachar banu mikol am, v'rom'manu mikal lashon,
v'kid'shanu b'mitzvotav. Vateetayn lanu, Adonai Elohaynu
b'ahavah, et yom** *(hashabbbat hazeh, v'et yom)* **hazika-ron
hazeh, yom** *(zichron)* **teruah,** *(b'ahavah)* **mikrah kodesh,
zaycher leey'tzi-at mitzrayim. Ki vanu vacharta, v'otanu
keedashta, mikal ha-amim, ud'varcha emet v'kayam la-ad.
Baruch atah Adonai, melech al kol ha-aretz,
m'ka-daysh** *(hashabbat v')* **Yisrael v'yom hazikaron.** *Listeners
respond* Amen.

When Rosh Hashanah *falls on Saturday evening, a candle*
with at least two wicks touching each other is held
and the following blessings are added.

**Baruch atah Adonai, Elohaynu melech ha-olam,
boray m'oray ha-aysh.** *Listeners respond* Amen *and everyone brings
their fingers near the flame to see the flame reflected in their fingernails.*

**Baruch atah Adonai, Elohaynu melech ha-olam,
hamavdil bayn kodesh l'chol, bayn ohr l'cho-shech,
bayn Yisrael la-amim, bayn yom hash'vee-ee l'shay-shet**

y'may hama-aseh, bayn k'dushat Shabbat lik'dushat
Yom Tov hivdalta, v'et yom hash'vee-ee mee-shayshet
y'may hama-aseh keedashta, hivdalta v'keedashta et
amcha Yisrael bik'du-sha-techa.
Baruch atah Adonai, hamavdil bayn kodesh l'kodesh.
Listeners respond Amen.

**Baruch atah Adonai, Elohaynu melech ha-olam,
she-heh-che-yanu, v'keey'manu, v'heegee-anu,
lazman hazeh.** *Listeners respond* Amen.

⚛ CONCLUDING HYMNS ☙

ALAYNU
("It is our duty")

For the last 700 years this has been the final hymn of each of
the daily prayers including Festival and Sabbath prayers. Rabbi
Hai Ben David Gaon in the 9th century wrote that this sublime
prayer was composed by Joshua as he brought his people into
the promised land. Similar to the *Shema*, it is a declaration of
faith and also expresses our gratitude for being able to serve
G-d. Throughout the centuries, *Alaynu* was prohibited or
censored in many countries. In particular the line in *Alaynu*
stating "they bow to vanity and emptiness. . ." was considered
an attack on other religions and was censored in Europe. It is
still omitted from many prayer books.

> **A 84 BC 43 B 43 M 59 L 36**

**Alaynu l'shabayach la-adon hakol, latayt g'dula l'yotzayr
b'raysheet. Shelo asanu k'goyay ha-aratzot, v'lo samanu
k'mishpechot ha-adama. Sheh-lo sam chelkaynu
kahem,v'goralaynu k'chol hamonam.** *(bow knees and head
for the following underlined words)* **Va-anachnu <u>kor'im</u>
<u>umishta-chavim</u> umodim, lifnay melech malchay
ham'lachim, Hakadosh Baruch Hu.**

**Shehu noteh shamayim v'yosed aretz, umoshav y'karo
bashamayim mima-al, u'shchinat uzo b'govhay m'romim.**

Hu Elohaynu, ayn od. Emet malkaynu, efes zulato, ka-
katuv b'torato v'yadata hayom va-hashay-vota el
l'vavecha, ki Adonai hu ha-Elohim bashamayim mima-al,
v'al ha-aretz mitachat ayn od.

This is the last verse of the second section of Alaynu.
In many synagogues, the Chazan and Cong. sing this verse together.

V'ne-emar, v'haya Adonai, l'melech al kol ha-aretz,
bayom ha-hu yihyeh Adonai echad ush'mo echad.

℘ KADDISH YATOM ℘
("Mourner's *Kaddish*")

The *Mourner's Kaddish* is recited at every service for
eleven months after the death of a parent. It is also recited
on the yearly anniversary *(Yahrtzeit)* of the death. *Kaddish*
is a source of merit for the soul. Although this prayer makes
no mention of the deceased, it serves an important role for
the mourner. Reciting a prayer in public helps to bring the
mourner back within the community. It also affirms for the
mourner a belief in G-d's righteousness. The most important
part is the response: *Amen, Y'hay sh'may rabbah m'varach . . .*
("May His great name be blessed forever and ever.")

A 86	BC 45	B 45	M 61	L 37

Mourner recites.

Yitgadal, v'yitkadash, sh'may rabbah. *Cong. responds* Amen.
B'almah di-v'ra chirutay, v'yamlich malchutay,
b'chayaychon uv'yomaychon, u'v'chayay d'chol
bayt Yisrael, ba-agalah uvizman kareev,
v'imru, Amen. *Cong. responds* Amen.

Chazan and Cong. recite together: Y'hay sh'may rabbah m'varach,
l'alam ul'almay almayah.

Yitbarach, v'yishtabach, v'vit-pa-ar, v'yit-romam,
v'yit-naseh, v'yit-hadar, v'yit-aleh, v'yit-halal,
sh'may d'kudshah, B'rich Hu. *Cong. responds* B'rich Hu.

L'aylah, l'aylah, mikol birchatah v'shiratah,

tushb'chatah, v'ne-chematah, da-amiran b'almah,
v'imru, **Amen.** *Cong. responds* Amen.

Y'hay shlamah rabbah min sh'mayah, v'chayim,
alaynu v'al kol Yisrael, v'imru, **Amen.** *Cong. responds* Amen.

Oseh hashalom bimromav, hu ya-aseh shalom,
alaynu v'al kol Yisrael, v'imru, **Amen.** *Cong. responds* Amen.

L'DAVID, ADONAI ORI V'YISHEE
("Of David, G-d is my light and redeemer")

> **A 86 BC 45 B 45 M 62 L —**

This psalm contains allusions to the entire Holiday season and is especially appropriate during the Days of Awe. It expresses our faith in G-d and our longing to be closer to Him. The Mourner's *Kaddish* follows, please see page 14.

CUSTOMS VARY REGARDING CONCLUDING
HYMNS. SOME SYNAGOGUES RECITE *ADON*
OLAM, OTHERS CONCLUDE WITH *YIGDAL*.

ADON OLAM
("Eternal Lord")

This hymn expresses our absolute trust in G-d's omnipotence and permanence. While *Olam* can mean both eternity and world, here it is generally understood to refer to the eternity of the Lord.

Adon Olam has been attributed to various medieval poets, and was most likely written by the Spanish poet Solomon Ibn Gabriol in the 11th century, although it may date back to Babylonian times.

> **A 88 BC 53 B 53 M 66 L 49**

Cong. and Chazan *sing together.*

Adon olam asher malach, b'terem kol yetzir nivrah,
L'ayt na-a-sa b'cheftzo kol, ahzay melech sh'mo nikrah.

V'acharay kichlot ha-kol, l'vado yimloch norah,
V'hu haya v'hu hoveh, v'hu yihyeh b'tifarah.

V'hu echad, v'ayn shaynee, l'hamsheel lo l'hachbirah,
B'li raysheet, b'li tachlit, v'lo ha-ohz v'hamisrah.

V'hu ayli, v'chai go-ali, v'tzur chevli b'ayt tzarah,
V'hu neesi u-manos li, m'nat kosi b'yom ekrah.

B'yado afkid ruchi, b'ayt eeshan v'ah-eerah,
V'im ruchi g'viyati, Adonai li v'lo eerah.

YIGDAL
("Exalted")

Yigdal, like *Shema* and *Alaynu*, summarizes the basic Jewish credo of monotheism. *Yigdal* also contains the Thirteen Principles of [the Jewish] Faith as defined by Maimonides.

A 88 BC 55 B 55 M 75 L —

Cong. and Chazan *sing together:*

Yigdal Elohim chai, v'yishtabach,
　　nimtza v'ayn et, el mitzee-uto.
Echad v'ayn yachid, k'yee-chudo,
　　ne-elam v'gam ayn sof, l'achduto.
Ayn lo d'mut haguf, v'ayno guf,
　　lo na-aroch aylav, k'dushato.
Kadmon l'chol davar, asher nivra,
　　rishon v'ayn raysheet, l'raysheeto.
Hino adon olam, l'chol notzar,
　　yoreh g'dulato, umalchuto.
Shefa n'vu-ato, n'ta-no,
　　el anshay s'gulato, v'tifarto.
Lo kam b'Yisrael, k'Moshe od,
　　navee umah-beet, et t'munato.
Torat emet natan, l'amo El,
　　al yad n'vee-o, ne-eman bayto.
Lo yacha-leef ha-El, v'lo yamir dato,
　　l'olamim l'zulato.
Tzofeh v'yo-day-a, s'taraynu,
　　mahbeet l'sof davar, b'kadmato.
Gomel l'ish chesed, k'mifalo,
　　notayn l'rasha ra, k'rish-ato.
Yishlach l'kaytz hayamin, m'shee-chaynu,

lifdot m'cha-kay kaytz, y'shu-ato.
Maytim y'chayeh El, b'rov chasdo,
baruch aday ad, shem t'hilato.

After the Evening Service and *only* on the first night of *Rosh Hashanah*, one greets family members, friends and neighbors with a special blessing. "May you immediately be inscribed and sealed for a good year."

To a male: **L'Shanah Tovah Ti-ka-tayv v'tay-cha-taym (l'altar l'chayim tovim ul'shalom).**

To a female: **L'Shanah Tovah Ti-ka-tayvee v'tay-cha-taymee (l'altar l'chayim tovim ul'shalom).**

This heartfelt greeting is based on the Talmudic statement that "three books lie open before G-d on *Rosh Hashanah*. The righteous are immediately inscribed for good in the Book of Life. The wicked are immediately inscribed in the Book of Death. And those in balance must wait for the decree until after *Yom Kippur*" (*Rosh Hashanah* 16b).

This greeting is only applicable on the first night of *Rosh Hashanah,* since that is when the Books of Life are first opened. Since judgment only takes place during the day, it would be inappropriate to recite it at any other time. On other occasions during *Rosh Hashanah* and the entire holiday season, one greets his/her family, friends and neighbors with a simple *Gut Yahr* ("Good Year") or with heartfelt wishes for a happy, healthy and sweet New Year.

One leaves the synagogue in a joyous, yet somber, frame of mind, because of the awesomeness of *Rosh Hashanah*.

When we arrive home, we set the table, *Kiddush* is recited and we eat *challah* and an apple dipped in honey symbolizing our wishes for a sweet year. A short blessing is recited prior to partaking of each of the symbolic foods (see introduction). Please consult the *machzor* for these blessings.

❦ The Winter Coat ❧

I n the 18th century, Rabbi Yaakov Ben Z'ev Kranz, known as the *Maggid* (preacher) of Dubno used to tell this story:

A poor man desperately needed a winter coat. He went to a major avenue and stood on a street corner begging for days until he had collected enough money. At the coat store he took the shopkeeper aside and explained how poor he was. He tried his best to convince the shopkeeper to give him a coat free of charge. The store owner took pity on him and gave him the coat. To the shopkeeper's surprise, the poor man handed him a handful of money—all the money he had collected.

After the poor man left the store, his daughter said to him, "Father, why did you ask for the coat for free, if you meant to pay?"

The poor man said, "I was afraid I still wouldn't have enough. As long as I knew the shopkeeper was kind enough to give me the coat for nothing, I knew any money I could give him would be acceptable."

The *Maggid* said: This is why we do not approach G-d on The Day of Judgement announcing our good deeds—for who has done enough good deeds to pay for all the mercy that G-d has already shown us? We can offer nothing, but we can hope and pray for His charity and that he will give us His blessings for nothing. Only then do we offer him what little we have, and hope that it will be acceptable to Him.

Shacharit
The Morning Service

hacharit is the Morning Service (from the Hebrew word meaning "dawn"). It includes morning blessings, psalms of praise, the *Shema* and *Shemoneh Esray* and is embellished with many *piyutim (liturgical poems)*.

✷ BIRCHOT HASHACHAR ✷
("Morning Blessings")

A 182 BC 51 B 51 M 74 L 45

Every morning when we wake up we express our gratitude to G-d, thanking Him for restoring our souls and our strength for another day.

This portion of the service consists of meditation and prayerful thoughts, recited informally in the home or in the synagogue. Several prayers deal with rising in the morning, washing the hands, personal hygiene, and moral and ethical concerns. In these blessings, we thank G-d for the mundane aspects of our lives which are normally taken for granted. Selections from the *Torah* and the *Talmud* recall many of the *Korbanot* ("sacrifices") which were offered to G-d at the time the Temple stood.

☙ P'SUKAY D'ZIMRAH ☜

("Psalms of Praise")

```
A 220 BC 133  B 133  M 120  L 59
```

After we thank G-d for granting us another day, we praise Him, describing His majesty and glory as the Creator of heaven and earth and the Creator of all creatures.

This section consists of a beautiful series of chapters mostly from the Psalms (many written by King David), praising G-d's name and His sovereignty, and describing the glory of G-d that surrounds us, as we prepare to say the *Shema* and *Shemoneh Esray*. The Psalms of Praise begin with a blessing, *Baruch She-amar* ("Blessed is He Who spoke") and conclude with a blessing, *Yishtabach* ("May [Your Name] be praised").

Some of the more important prayers in this section are:

BARUCH SHE-AMAR

("Blessed is He Who spoke")

According to tradition, the Rabbis of the Sanhedrin were Divinely inspired when they wrote this poetic introduction, which blesses seven aspects of G-d.

```
A 222 BC 135  B 135  M 124  L 70
```

Cong. and Chazan *softly in unison.*

Baruch she-amar v'hayah ha-olam, Baruch hu.
Baruch oseh v'ray-sheet, Baruch omayr v'oseh,
Baruch gozayr um'kayaym, Baruch m'ra-chaym al ha-aretz.
Baruch m'rachaym al habri-ot,
Baruch m'sha-laym sachar tov leey'ray-av,
Baruch chai la-ad, v'kayam la-netzach,
Baruch podeh uma-tzeel, Baruch sh'mo.
Baruch atah Adonai, Elohaynu melech ha-olam,
ha-El, ha-av ha-rachaman, ham'hulal b'feh amo,
m'shu-bach um'fo-ar bilshon chasidav va-avadav,
u'v'shee-ray David av-de-chah,

**n'halel-chah Adonai Elohaynu bishvachot, uvizmirot,
n'gadel-chah un'sha-bay-cha-chah, un'fa-er-chah,
v'naz-kir shimchah, v'namlee-ch'chah, malkaynu, Elohaynu.
Yachid chay ha-olamim, melech, m'shubach um'fo-ar,
ah-day ad sh'mo ha-gadol.
Baruch atah Adonai, melech m'hulal batish-ba-chot.**

MIZMOR SHIR
("A song [for the Sabbath]")

A 242 BC 151 B 151 M 147 L 70

The *Levites* sang this psalm at the Sabbath Temple Service. It praises G-d and the Sabbath day and describes the tranquility brought about by our realization of the justice and kindness of G-d's ways.

ASHRAY
("Fortunate")

A 244 BC 153 B 153 M 152 L 71

This psalm contains most of the letters of the alphabet symbolizing that we praise G-d with everything at our disposal and that G-d takes care of each and every form of life. The psalm extols G-d's virtues and His intimate involvement in the world. This psalm is considered of great significance. The Rabbis of the Talmud declared that those who recite this psalm three times daily will be assured a part of in the World to Come.

NISHMAT

A 258 BC 165 B 165 M 170 L 77

("The soul [of every living thing]")
Our complete dependency on G-d is described in this moving prayer. We again express praise and gratitude to G-d for all the myriads of things He has done for us.

HAMELECH
("O King")

Day 1	A 262	BC 169	B 169	M 175	L 80
Day 2	A 262	BC 169	B 431	M 451	L 80

The prayer affirms G-d, King of Kings, who sits on His great throne. The *Chazan* chants the haunting melody of this prayer. He begins several steps away from the *Amud* (place where he leads the congregation), to indicate his reverence. This section ends with the recital of the final paragraph of the Psalms of Praise, *Yishtabach*.

YISHTABACH
("May Your Name be praised")

Day 1	A 264	BC 169	B 169	M 176	L 81
Day 2	A 264	BC 169	B 431	M 452	L 81

This concluding blessing of the Psalms of Praise contains fifteen praises of G-d and declares that as much as we have lauded Him, He is, in fact, far greater than can ever be described.

The Congregation rises and together with the Chazan *recites this softly.*

Yishtabach shimchah la-ad malkaynu,
ha-el hamelech hagadol v'hakadosh,
bashamayim, uva-aretz.
Ki le-chah na-eh Adonai Elohaynu, vaylohay
avotaynu, shir ush'vacha, hallel v'zimrah,
oz umemshalah, netzach, g'dulah ug'vurah,
t'hilah v'tiferet, k'dushah umalchut,
B'rachot, v'hoda-ot, may-atah v'ad olam.
Baruch atah Adonai, El, melech, gadol
batish-bachot, El hahoda-ot, adon hanifla-ot,
habo-chayr b'sheeray zimrah,
melech, El, chay ha-olamim.

SHIR HAMA-ALOT
("A Song of Ascents")

In this psalm, recited by the *Levites* as they ascended the 15 steps to the Temple's sanctuary, we ask G-d for forgiveness and express our yearning to be close to Him. Finally, we ask G-d for redemption.

THE *ARON* IS OPENED.

Day 1	A 264	BC 171	B 171	M 176	L 81
Day 2	A 264	BC 171	B 433	M 453	L 81

Chazan *recites each line, Cong. repeats.*

Shir hama-alot, mi-ma-amakim k'raticha Adonai.
Adonai shim-a b'koli, tih-yeh-na aznecha kashuvot,
   l'kol tacha-nunai.
Im avonot tishmor yah, Adonai mi ya-amod.
Ki imcha haselichah, l'ma-an tivareh.
Keeveeti Adonai, kivtah nafshi, v'lidvaro hochalti.
Nafshi l'Adonai mishomrim laboker, shomrim laboker.
Yachayl Yisrael el Adonai, ki im Adonai hachesed,
   v'harbeh imo f'doot.
V'hu yifdeh et Yisrael, mikol avonotav.

THE *ARON* IS CLOSED.

⛭ THE HALF *KADDISH* ❧

In this beautiful and ancient prayer we ask that G-d's name be exalted throughout the world. The Congregation should recite the appropriate responses with concentration and devotion, especially *Amen, Y'hay sh'may rabbah m'varach* . . . ("May His great name be blessed forever and ever").

Day 1	A 264	BC 171	B 171	M 177	L 82
Day 2	A 264	BC 171	B 433	M 453	L 82

Chazan *recites:*

Yitgadal, v'yitkadash, sh'may rabbah. *Cong. responds* Amen.
B'almah di-v'ra chirutay, v'yamlich malchutay,
b'chayaychon uv'yomaychon, u'v'chayay d'chol

bayt Yisrael, ba-agalah uvizman kareev,
v'imru, **Amen.** *Cong. responds* Amen.

Chazan and Cong. recite together: **Y'hay sh'may rabbah
m'varach, l'alam ul'almay almayah.**

**Yitbarach, v'yishtabach, v'yit-pa-ar, v'yit-romam,
v'yit-naseh, v'yit-hadar, v'yit-aleh, v'yit-halal,
sh'may d'kudshah, B'rich Hu.** *Cong. responds* B'rich Hu.

**L'aylah, l'aylah, mikol birchatah v'shiratah,
tushb'chatah, v'ne-chematah, da-amiran b'almah,
v'imru, Amen.** *Cong. responds* Amen.

☞ BARCHU ☜
(Invitation to Congregation to Bless G-d)
The *Chazan* summons the Congregation to bless G-d, which
is followed by the Congregational response.

Day 1	A 266	BC 171	B 171	M 178	L 82
Day 2	A 266	BC 171	B 433	M 454	L 82

The Chazan *and Cong. bow slightly at the command* Barchu *and
everyone stands erect when G-d's name is recited.*

Chazan **Barchu Et Adonai Ham-vorach**

Everyone again bows at the word Baruch *and straightens up at G-d's name.*

Cong. **Baruch Adonai Ham-vorach L'olam Va-ed**

This sentence is repeated by the Chazan.

☞ THE SHEMA AND ITS BLESSINGS ☜
The *Shema* is an affirmation of the Oneness of G-d and our
acceptance of His commandments. Because we are inspired
by G-d's goodness and love, after thanking Him and praising
Him, we now declare His absolute sovereignty, and accept
upon ourselves the commitment to observe His commandments.

Following *Barchu* we recite two blessings that precede the
Shema: *Yotzayr Ohr* ("Who Creates the Luminaries") and
Ahavah Rabbah ("[with] abundant love"). Within *Yotzayr
Ohr* are several liturgical poems (*piyutim*) expressing the spirit
of the day, e.g., Kingship and Forgiveness, which are written
in various alphabetical arrangements.

[If Rosh Hashana falls on Shabbat, many prayers are said in addition to the hymn El Adon.]

WHEN *ROSH HASHANAH* FALLS ON A WEEKDAY,
PLEASE CONTINUE TO THE FOLLOWING PAGE.

EL ADON
("G-d, the Master")

A 280 BC 185 B 179 M 184 L 83

This alphabetically arranged poem praises G-d's greatness, with special emphasis on the heavenly bodies.

Chazan and Cong. recite or sing together.

El Adon al kol ha-ma-asim,
Baruch um'vorach b'fi kol neshamah,
Gadlo v'tuvo maleh olam,
Da-at utevunah sovevim oto.

Hamitgah-eh al chayot hakodesh,
V'ne-he-dar b'chavod al hamerkavah,
Z'chut umishor lifnay chis-oh,
Chesed v'rachamim lifnay ch'vodo.

Tovim m'o-rot she-barah Elohaynu,
Yetzaram b'da-at b'vinah u'v'haskayl,
Ko-ach ug'vurah natan bahem,
Lihyot moshlim b'kerev tayvayl.

M'layim ziv u'm'fikim nogah,
Na-eh zivam b'chol ha-olam,
S'maychim b'tzaytam v'sasim b'vo-am,
Osim b'aymah r'tzon konam.

P'er v'chavod notnim lishmo,
Tzahalah v'reenah l'zaycher malchuto,
Karah la-shemesh vayizrach ohr,
Ra-ah v'hitkin tzurat hal'vanah.

She-vach notnim lo,
Kol tz'vah mahrom,
Tiferet ug'dulah,
Serafim v'ofanim v'chayot hakodesh.

𝒞 KEDUSHAH 🕊

Following the praises of G-d as the Creator of all things, we recite the Modified *Kedushah*, the song in which the angels proclaim the holiness and kingship of G-d.

Day 1	A 284	BC 189	B 183	M 188	L 85
Day 2	A 284	BC 189	B 443	M 460	L 85

Cong. and Chazan *in unison.*

Kadosh, Kadosh, Kadosh, Adonai Tz'va-ot, Meloh Chol Ha-aretz K'vodo.

("Holy, Holy, Holy is the G-d of hosts; the whole earth is full of His glory.")

Day 1	A 288	BC 191	B 185	M 189	L 85
Day 2	A 288	BC 191	B 445	M 461	L 85

The following may not be said immediately but only after the the recital of a few piyutim.

Cong. and Chazan *in unison.*

Baruch K'vod Adonai Mimkomo.

("Blessed is the glory of G-d from His place")

BLESSINGS OF THE SHEMA

Day 1	A 288	BC 193	B 187	M 189	L 85
Day 2	A 288	BC 193	B 447	M 461	L 85

The first blessing, *Yotzayr Ohr* ("Who Creates the Luminaries") is lengthy and praises G-d for creating the heavenly bodies and the angels. It concludes with the words *Yotzayr Ham'orot* ("Who Creates the Luminaries"), after which the Congregation responds *Amen*.

Ahavah Rabbah ("[with] abundant love") is the second blessing, and it is said just prior to reciting the *Shema*. In this blessing we thank G-d for the *Torah* and pray for the wisdom to understand and observe it. We also plead that G-d will gather us from everywhere on earth and return us to our Holy Land. It concludes with the words *Habo-chayr B'amo Yisrael B'ahavah* ("Who chooses His people Israel with love"), after which the Congregation responds *Amen*.

THE SHEMA
(Acceptance of G-d's sovereignty)

Day 1	A 290	BC 195	B 189	M 193	L 86
Day 2	A 290	BC 195	B 449	M 465	L 86

Chazan *and Cong. recite aloud, carefully enunciating each word.*

Shema Yisrael, Adonai Elohaynu, Adonai Echad.

The first passage (*Deuteronomy* 6:4) and the three paragraphs that follow are part of both the daily morning and evening worship services. The *Shema* is the most important single sentence in the liturgy, for it is not a prayer but rather an affirmation that G-d is One. It is the Jew's confession of faith and many martyrs have died with this prayer on their lips. The *Shema* is so important and so well summarizes the basic tenets of Judaism that its first two paragraphs are inscribed on the scrolls of both the *mezuzah* and *tefillin*.

It is important to concentrate fully on all three paragraphs, because the recitation of the *Shema* represents the acceptance of G-d's absolute sovereignty.

For men wearing the *Tallit*, the four corners are gathered together prior to the recital of the *Shema* and held in the left hand between one's last two fingers. At the mention of the word *Tzitzit* in the final paragraph, the *Tzitzit* are moved to the right hand and kissed. At the last word of the *Shema—Emet*, the *Tzitzit* are again kissed. *(For additional explanation and a complete transliteration of the* Shema, *please refer to the Evening Service, pages 3—6.)*

CONCLUDING BLESSING OF THE *SHEMA*

Day 1	A 292	BC 197	B 191	M 198	L 88
Day 2	A 292	BC 197	B 451	M 470	L 88

As we prepare for the Silent Devotion, we recite the final blessing, *Ga-al Yisrael*, which elaborates on the exodus from Egypt and concludes with a plea that G-d manifest himself again and redeem Israel from exile.

The Cong. rises in preparation for the Shemoneh Esray, *the Silent Devotion.*

MI CHAMOCHAH
("Who is like You")

Day 1 A 296	BC 199	B 193	M 202	L 89
Day 2 A 296	BC 199	B 453	M 474	L 89

Chazan and Cong. recite or sing together.

Mi chamochah ba-aylim Adonai,
mi kamochah ne-edar bakodesh,
norah t'hilot o-seh feleh.

ADONAI YIMLOCH
("God will reign")

Adonai Yimloch L'olam Va-ed.
Tzur Yisrael, kumah b'ezrat Yisrael,
u'f'day chinu-mechah Yehudah v'Yisrael.
Go-alaynu Adonai tz'va-ot sh'mo k'dosh Yisrael.
Baruch atah Adonai, Ga-al Yisrael.

☜ SHEMONEH ESRAY ☞
(Silent Devotion to G-d)

Day 1 A 296	BC 201	B 195	M 203	L 89
Day 2 A 296	BC 201	B 455	M 475	L 89

Having thanked G-d, praised G-d, and accepted His commandments, we can now approach Him, offering further praise, and submitting our requests, both personal and communal. Finally we offer our thanks for His blessings.

The *Amida* or *Shemoneh Esray* is the same as in the Evening Service of *Rosh Hashanah. (For additional explanation, please refer to pages 9 and 60)*

☜ CHAZARAT HASHATZ ☞
("*Chazan's* Repetition")

Day 1 A 306	BC 209	B 203	M 217	L 95
Day 2 A 342	BC 229	B 463	M 488	L 95

The public repetition by the Chazan of the *Amida* forms an important part of the service, especially on the High

Holidays. Numerous liturgical poems (*piyutim*) underline the main theme of the Ten Days of Awe — G-d, as the King of the Universe, sitting in Divine judgment.

Several of *Rosh Hashanah*'s most important prayers are included, as well as additional hymns in this communal service. At various times the *Aron* is opened, and it is proper at such times to rise.

The *Chazan*'s repetition for each of the two days is slightly different; therefore please note the changes in the pages for each particular day. At the beginning of the repetition, the *Chazan* recites a special supplication, in which he beseeches G-d to hear his prayers on behalf of the Congregation. On the first day he recites *Ya-rayti Biftzoti* ("I am frightened") describing how lacking in good deeds he is and how afraid he is to even hope that G-d will accept his prayers. On the second day he recites a similar plea—*Ati-ti L'chan'nach* ("I come to beg of you").

Some of the more significant prayers:

✽ FIRST DAY OF ROSH HASHANAH ✽

FOR THE SECOND DAY OF *ROSH HASHANAH*, SEE PAGE 32.

ATAH HU ELOHAYNU
("Only G-d is our G-d")

This alphabetically arranged *piyut* describes the power and sovereignty of G-d. *Rosh Hashanah* is dedicated to the proclamation that G-d is our King and He is righteous and fair, close to all who sincerely call on Him.

THE *ARON* IS OPENED.

A 314 BC 217 B 211 M 221 L 98

Chazan *recites, Cong. repeats.*

Atah Hu Elohaynu.

B'shamayim uva-aretz, Gibor v'na-aratz.

Cong. *recites,* Chazzan. *repeats.*

Dagul mayr'vavah, Hu sach vayehi.

V'tzeevah v'nivra-oo,	Zichro lanetzach.
Chai olamim,	T'hor ay-na-yim.
Yoshayv sayter,	Kitro y'shu-ah.
L'vusho tz'dakah,	Ma-atayhu kin-ah.
Ne-epad n'kamah,	Sitro yosher.
Atzato emunah,	P'ulato emet.
Tzadik v'yashar,	Karov likor-av b'emet.
Ram umitnaseh,	Shochayn sh'chakim.
Toleh eretz al blimah.	

Chai, V'kayam, Norah, Umarom, V'kadosh.

THE *ARON* IS CLOSED.

VARIOUS *PIYUTIM* WILL BE SAID BY THE CONGREGATION
BEFORE THE RECITAL OF *ADONAI MELECH.*

ADONAI MELECH
("G-d Reigns")

This acrostic poem expresses the central themes of *Rosh Hashanah* —the oneness of G-d and His eternal Kingship. Both the angels above and the Children of Israel below joyously proclaim the unity and sovereignty of G-d—with the refrain, "G-d reigns, G-d has reigned, G-d will reign for eternity." This poem is recited on both days with slightly different arrangements.

THE *ARON* IS OPENED.
The first four stanzas have been transliterated since usually only these are sung aloud.

A 328 BC 225 B 229 M 228 L 101

Chazan *recites,* Cong. *repeats.*
Adonai Melech, Adonai Malach, Adonai Yimloch L'olam Va-ed.

Adeeray ayumah, ya-diru v'kol,

Cong. *recites each verse,* Chazan *repeats.*
Adonai Melech. B'ru-ay varak, y'varchu v'kol,
Adonai Malach. Gee-borai go-vah, yagbiru v'kol,
Adonai Yimloch.

Adonai Melech, Adonai Malach, Adonai Yimloch L'olam Va-ed.

Doha-ray dolkim, y'dov'vu v'kol,
Adonai Melech. Hamo-nay hamulah, y'halelu v'kol,
Adonai Malach. Va-chaya-lim v'chayot, y'va-adu v'kol,
        Adonai Yimloch.
Adonai Melech, Adonai Malach, Adonai Yimloch L'olam Va-ed.

Zoch-ray z'mirot, y'zamru v'kol,
Adonai Melech. Chach-may chidot, y'chas'nu v'kol,
Adonai Malach. Tafs'ray t'fuchim, y'taksu v'kol,
        Adonai Yimloch.
Adonai Melech, Adonai Malach, Adonai Yimloch L'olam Va-ed.

Yor-shay y'karah, yay'shiru v'kol,
Adonai Melech. Kabee-ray cho-ach, yachtiru v'kol,
Adonai Malach. L'voo-shay leha-vot y'lab'vu v'kol,
        Adonai Yimloch.
Adonai Melech, Adonai Malach, Adonai Yimloch L'olam Va-ed.

Please consult your Machzor *for the balance of the poem.*

THE *ARON* IS CLOSED.

L'EL ORECH DIN
("To G-d in Judgment")

This alphabetically arranged *piyut* is really a continuation of the previous *piyut*. It praises the attributes of G-d as He sits in judgment and is filled with forgiveness, compassion and mercy. Every first half-line ends with the words *B'yom Din* ("On the day of judgment"); the other half-line ends with the word *Badin* ("With judgment"). The poem is chanted with intense feeling, so that we can loudly and communally proclaim each of G-d's attributes.

THE *ARON* IS OPENED.

A 330 BC 261 B 233 M 232 L 105

Chazan *recites, Cong. repeats.*

Uv'chayn l'chah hakol yachtiru, L'el orech din.

Cong. recites, Chazan repeats.

L'vochen l'vavot,	b'yom din,
l'goleh amukot,	badin.
L'dovayr maysharim,	b'yom din,
l'hogeh day-ot,	badin.
L'vatik v'oseh chesed,	b'yom din,
l'zochayr b'rito,	badin.
L'chomayl ma-asav,	b'yom din,
l'ta-hayr cho-sav,	badin.
L'yoday-a machshavot,	b'yom din,
l'cho-vaysh ka-aso,	badin.
L'lovaysh tz'dakot,	b'yom din,
l'mochayl avonot,	badin.
L'norah t'hilot,	b'yom din,
l'solayach lamusav,	badin.
L'oneh l'kor'av,	b'yom din,
l'fo-ayl rachamav,	badin.
L'tzofeh nistarot,	b'yom din,
l'koneh avadav,	badin.
L'rachem amo,	b'yom din,
l'shomayr ohavav,	badin.
L'tomaych t'mimav,	b'yom din.

THE *ARON* IS CLOSED.

ON THE FIRST DAY OF *ROSH HASHANAH*, PLEASE
CONTINUE WITH THE *KEDUSHAH* PAGE 35.

✒ SECOND DAY OF ROSH HASHANAH ✒

ATAH HU ELOHAYNU

("Only G-d is our G-d")

This *piyut*, alphabetically arranged, describes the power and sovereignty of G-d. *Rosh Hashanah* is dedicated to the proclamation that G-d is our King and He is close to all who sincerely call on Him. This poem is also recited on the first day.

THE *ARON* IS OPENED.

A 352   BC 239   B 475   M 494   L 98

Chazan *recites, Cong. repeats.*

Atah Hu Elohaynu.
B'shamayim uva-aretz,   Gibor v'na-aratz.

Chazan *recites, Cong. repeats.*

Dagul mayr'vavah,	**Hu sach vayehi.**
V'tzeevah v'nivra-oo,	**Zichro lanetzach.**
Chai olamim,	**T'hor ay-na-yim.**
Yoshayv sayter,	**Kitro y'shu-ah.**
L'vusho tz'dakah,	**Ma-atayhu kin-ah.**
Ne-epad n'kamah,	**Sitro yosher.**
Atzato emunah,	**P'ulato emet.**
Tzadik v'yashar,	**Karov likor-av b'emet.**
Ram umitnaseh,	**Shochayn sh'chakim.**
Toleh eretz al blimah.	

Chai, V'kayam, Norah, Umarom, V'kadosh.

THE *ARON* IS CLOSED.

VARIOUS *PIYUTIM* ARE SAID BY THE
CONGREGATION BEFORE *MELECH ELYON*

MELECH ELYON
("The Supreme King")

This prayer is an affirmation of G-d's boundless majesty. We extol His greatness, and as in many of the prayers of *Rosh Hashanah*, G-d is acknowledged as our Eternal King. Each sentence ends with the statement *La-adai Ad Yimloch Melech Elyon* ("Forever shall He reign, the Supreme King.") This poem is recited on the second day during the *Shacharit* Service and a similar version on the first day during the *Mussaf* Service.

THE *ARON* IS OPENED.

The first four stanzas have been transliterated since usually only these are sung aloud.

| A 366 | BC 251 | B 493 | M 501 | L 101 |

Chazan *recites,* Cong. *repeats.*

**Uv'chayn vayhee veeshu-roon Melech,
Melech Elyon.**

Cong. *recites,* Chazan *repeats.*

**Amitz ham'nusa, l'chal rosh mitna-say,
omayr v'oseh, ma-oz umach-seh,
nisah v'nosay, moshiv m'lachim la-kisay,
La-aday Ad Yimloch, Melech Elyon.**

**Gibor big'vurot, koray hadorot,
goleh nistarot, imrotav t'horot,
yo-day-ah s'forot, l'to-tza-ot mazorot,
La-aday Ad Yimloch, Melech Elyon.**

**Ham'fo-ar b'fee chol, v'hu kol yachol,
ham'ra-chaym et kol, v'no-tayn michyah lakol,
v'ne-elam may-ayn kol, v'ay-nav m'shot'tot bakol,
La-aday Ad Yimloch, Melech Elyon.**

**Zo-chayr nish-ka-chot, cho-kayr tu-chot,
ay-nav p'ku-chot, magid say-chot,
Elohay ha-ru-chot, imro-tav n'cho-chot,
La-aday Ad Yimloch, Melech Elyon.**

Please consult your Machzor *for the balance of the poem.*

THE *ARON* IS CLOSED.

ADONAI MELECH
("G-d Reigns")

This acrostic poem expresses the central themes of *Rosh Hashanah*—the oneness of G-d and His eternal Kingship. Both the angels above and the Children of Israel below loudly proclaim the unity and sovereignty of G-d. This poem is recited on both days in a slightly different arrangement.

THE *ARON* IS OPENED.

The first four stanzas have been transliterated since usually only these are sung aloud.

A 370   BC 255   B 497   M 505   L 103

Chazan *recites, Cong. repeats.*

Adonai Melech, Adonai Malach, Adonai Yimloch L'olam Va-ed.

Kol shin-a-nay, sha-chak b'omer ma-adirim,

Cong. recites each verse, Chazan *repeats.*

Adonai Melech. Kol shoch-nay sheket, biv'racha m'varchim,
Adonai Malach. Aylu va-aylu, b'govah mag-dilim,
Adonai Yimloch.
Adonai Melech, Adonai Malach, Adonai Yimloch L'olam Va-ed.

Kol malachay maalah, b'day-ah mad-gilim,
Adonai Melech. Kol moshlay ma-tah, b'halel m'hal'lim,
Adonai Malach. Aylu va-aylu, b'vadai modim,
Adonai Yimloch.
Adonai Melech, Adonai Malach, Adonai Yimloch L'olam Va-ed.

Kol aree-tzay elyonim, b'zemer m'zamrim,
Adonai Melech. Kol ov-ray olamim, b'chayil m'chasnim,
Adonai Malach. Aylu va-aylu, b'ta-am m'taksim,
Adonai Yimloch.
Adonai Melech, Adonai Malach, Adonai Yimloch L'olam Va-ed.

Kol v'ooday va-ad, b'yosher m'yapim,
Adonai Melech. Kol vateekay veset, b'chosher m'chal'lim,
Adonai Malach. Aylu va-aylu, b'lahag m'lahagim,
Adonai Yimloch.
Adonai Melech, Adonai Malach, Adonai Yimloch L'olam Va-ed.

Please consult your machzor *for the balance of the poem.*

THE *ARON* IS CLOSED.

☙ THE SERVICE CONTINUES FOR BOTH DAYS ☙
KEDUSHAH
(Sanctification of G-d's Name)

This is the most important part of the *Chazan*'s repetition.

🦅 *Avinu Malkaynu* 🦅

According to the *Talmud* (*Ta'anith* 25b), there was a drought in Israel in the 1st century. Rabbi Eliezer ordered fasts and public prayers and yet no rain fell. Rabbi Akiva stepped in front of the *Aron* ("Ark") and loudly recited a five-verse prayer: "Our Father, Our King, we have no King but Thee. Our Father, Our King, for Thy sake have mercy upon us." Rain fell immediately.

Since then Rabbi Akiva's prayer has become a feature of prayers for fasts and other times of tragedy or need. This series of stanzas, each beginning with *Avinu Malkaynu* ("Our Father, Our King"), is recited on *Rosh Hashanah*, *Yom Kippur* and the days in between.

Calling G-d both Father and King expresses the intimacy, as well as the awe, we feel in our relationship with Him. In this prayer, the notion of G-d as Father is placed before that of G-d as King because during times of need we appeal to G-d as his children. For there is no compassion greater than a parents compassion for his child.

Avinu Malkaynu was composed for a fast day in a time of distress and thus is not recited on the joyous day of Sabbath.

We recite *Avinu Malkaynu* after the *Shemoneh Esray*. Standing, with the *Aron* open, we say the verses with fervor. In most Congregations, the nine verses in the middle of the prayer are recited aloud by the *Chazan* and the Congregation. In some synagogues, the last verse is sung together by *Chazan* and Congregation, while in others it is recited quietly: "Our Father, Our King, be gracious with us and answer us, for we have no merits of our own. Deal with us in charity and kindness, and save us."

Relating the fact that even the angels in the highest of heavens praise G-d.

Day 1	A 374	BC 261	B 233	M 233	L 106
Day 2	A 374	BC 261	B 503	M 511	L 106

Cong. recites, Chazan *repeats.*

**N'kadaysh et shimchah ba-olam,
k'shaym sheh-makdishim oto, bishmay marom,
kakatoov al yad n'vee-echa,
v'karah zeh el zeh v'amar.**

Chazan *and Cong. recite together. We
rise on our toes when reciting the first three words*

**Kadosh, Kadosh, Kadosh, Adonai Tz'va-ot,
Meloh Chal Ha-aretz K'vodo.**

Cong. recites, Chazan *repeats.*

**Az b'kol, ra-ash gadol, adir v'chazak
mashmee-im kol, mit-nasim l'umat serafim,
l'umatam baruch yomayru.**

Chazan *and Cong. recite together. During the word* Baruch *we
rise on our toes.*

Baruch K'vod Adonai Mimkomo.

Cong. recites, Chazan *repeats.*

**Mimkomcha malkaynu toh-fee-ah,
v'timloch alaynu, ki m'chakim anachnu lach.
Matai timloch b'tziyon,
b'karov, b'yamaynu, l'olam va-ed tishkon.
Titgadal, v'titkadash, b'toch Yerushalayim irchah,
l'dor vador, ul'naytzach n'tzachim.
V'ayaynu tirehnah, malchu-techah,
kadavar ha-amur b'sheeray uzechah.
Al y'day David, m'shee-ach tzidkechah.**

Chazan *and Cong. recite together. During the word* Yimloch *we
rise on our toes.*

**Yimloch Adonai L'olam, Elohayich Tziyon,
L'dor Vador, Halleluyah.**

The *Chazan* continues the repetition of the *Shemoneh Esray* in the special High Holiday melody. The Congregation listens intently, answering *Amen* where applicable.

AVINU MALKAYNU
("Our Father, Our King")

At the conclusion of the *Chazan*'s repetition of the *Amida*, we recite this important prayer, a series of 44 verses of supplication. We ask G-d as both our Father and our King to be merciful with us. In the middle of the prayer, nine verses, particulary significant to the theme of the High Holidays, are recited by the *Chazan* and repeated by the Congregation. The last verse is usually sung together. [When *Rosh Hashanah* falls on the Sabbath, *Avinu Malkaynu* is not recited.]

Day 1	A 384	BC 271	B 243	M 244	L 110
Day 2	A 384	BC 271	B 513	M 521	L 110

THE *ARON* IS OPENED.

The following is an excerpt from the 15th to the 24th verse of Avinu Malkaynu.

Avinu Malkaynu, hacha-zee-raynu bit'shuvah sh'laymah l'fanecha.

Avinu Malkaynu, sh'lach r'fuah sh'laymah l'cholay amecha.

Avinu Malkaynu, k'ra ro-ah g'zar deenaynu.

Avinu Malkaynu, zachraynu b'zeekaron tov l'fanecha.

Avinu Malkaynu, katvaynu b'sefer chayim tovim.

Avinu Malkaynu, katvaynu b'sefer g'ulah veey'shuah.

Avinu Malkaynu, katvaynu b'sefer parnasah v'chalkalah.

Avinu Malkaynu, katvaynu b'sefer z'chuyot.

Avinu Malkaynu, katvaynu b'sefer s'lichah um'cheelah.

Last verse is usually sung in unison.

Avinu Malkaynu, chanaynu va-anaynu ki ayn banu ma-asim.

Aseh imanu, tz'dakah va-chesed, v'hoshiaynu.

THE *ARON* IS CLOSED.

⁊ KADDISH SHALAYM ☙
("Full *Kaddish*")

The final part of every Congregational Service is the Full *Kaddish,* wherein G-d's name is magnified and sanctified and we pray that our service will be accepted. The Congregation should recite the appropriate responses with concentration and devotion, especially *Amen, Y'hay sh'may rabbah m'varach . . .* ("May His great name be blessed forever and ever").

Day 1	A 388	BC 275	B 247	M 248	L 111
Day 2	A 388	BC 275	B 517	M 526	L 111

Chazan *recites:*

Yitgadal, v'yitkadash, sh'may rabbah. *Cong. responds* Amen.
B'almah di-v'ra chirutay, v'yamlich malchutay, b'chayaychon uv'yomaychon, u'v'chayay d'chol bayt Yisrael, ba-agalah uvizman kareev, v'imru, Amen. *Cong. responds* Amen.

Chazan *and Cong. recite together:* **Y'hay sh'may rabbah m'varach, l'alam ul'almay almayah.**

Yitbarach, v'yishtabach, v'yit-pa-ar, v'yit-romam, v'yit-naseh, v'yit-hadar, v'yit-aleh, v'yit-halal, sh'may d'kudshah, B'rich Hu. *Cong. responds* B'rich Hu.

L'aylah, l'aylah, mikol birchatah v'shiratah, tush-b'chatah, v'ne-chematah, da-amiran b'almah, v'imru, Amen. *Cong. responds* Amen.

Titkabel tz'lot-hon u-va-ut-hon d'chol bayt Yisrael, kadam avu-hon di vish-maya, v'imru, Amen. *Cong. responds* Amen.

Y'hay sh'lama rabbah min sh'maya, v'chayim, alaynu v'al kol Yisrael, v'imru, Amen. *Cong. responds* Amen.

Oseh hashalom bimro-mav, Hu ya-aseh shalom, alaynu v'al kol Yisrael, v'imru, Amen. *Cong. responds* Amen.

The Congregation stands, awaiting the opening of the Aron *and the removal of the* Torah *scrolls.*

⚘ *Listening to the Shofar* ☙

After the Spanish Inquisition, when many of the Jews remaining in Spain had to accept Christianity, they privately remained loyal to Judaism and secretly observed G-d's commandments. One of the great leaders of the time was Don Fernando Aguilar, conductor of the royal orchestra.

The Days of Awe were soon approaching, and the small community of Jews left in one Spanish town longed to hear the sound of the *shofar*. Don Fernando had an idea. He scheduled a concert featuring instrumental music. Many of those in attendance were these forcibly converted Jews. They came to listen to a concert and listen they did, for among the compositions were the sounds of the *shofar.*

Leading bishops and Christian emissaries were also present at the concert. They all heard but knew not. Only the Jews understood *"tekiah, shevarim, teruah..."* under the very direction of Don Fernando himself.

The inquisition unfortunately was not the first time, nor was it the last time, that Jews had to find an ingenious way to hear the *shofar*. There have been accounts of Jews risking their lives to hear the *shofar* throughout Jewish history. Yaffa Eliach recounts a number of these stories in her book, *Hasidic Tales of the Holocaust*. In one account she tells a story she heard of a man named Moshe in the concentration camp in Skarzysko. In 1943 he was given a ram's horn by Rabbi Yitzchak Finkler of Radorzyts who was a fellow inmate. The Rabbi asked Moshe to do the work necessary to turn the ram's horn into a *shofar*. Moshe spent days in the carpentry shop working on it. He finished his work on time, and on *Rosh Hashanah* the *shofar* was sounded by Rabbi Finkler in barrack 14. Rabbi Finkler was later murdered by the Nazis, but Moshe survived. The *shofar* somehow also survived and is now in the collection of the Yad Vashem museum in Jerusalem.

Kriyat Hatorah
The Torah Service

etween the Morning Service and *Mussaf* ("Additional Service") we read from the *Torah*.

A *Torah* scroll is the result of an exacting labor of love by a dedicated and specially trained scribe. For thousands of years the Hebrew calligraphy used to write these scrolls has been the same. There are laws regarding every detail of the scroll, from the preparation of the parchment (made from the hide of a kosher animal) to the ink and the shape of the letters. No vocalization, punctuation or musical notes appear in the text. The sexton of the synagogue or a trained layman reads the text following a cantillation method that has remained unchanged for more than two millennia.

The *Torah* is divided into 54 portions. Each year the cycle of reading in all synagogues is both completed and begun on the holiday of *Simchat Torah*. The weekly portion is called the *sedra* or *parsha*, and the name of each week's *sedra* usually comes from the first word of that portion. Because of the nature of the calendar, two *sedrot* are read together in certain weeks, in order to complete the cycle at the appropriate time. On holidays, portions from the *Torah* pertaining to the specific holiday are read.

The *Torah* scroll is dressed and decorated in a style reflecting the priestly dress of Temple times. A breastplate, robe and belt were all worn by the High Priest in Jerusalem. Since the destruction of the Temple in 70 C.E., we use the ancient symbols of priesthood to preserve a link with the past. The robe, mantle and belt of the scroll are usually made of the finest materials—velvet or silk magnificently embroidered by hand, with the breastplate made of ornate silver.

Males over the age of thirteen are involved in the *Torah* service by means of an *Aliyah* (literally, "Ascent"). This is an honor given to those who recite the blessings of the *Torah*. It is called *Aliyah* for two reasons. First one must literally ascend to the synagogue's elevated *bimah* ("platform"). Second, reading from the *Torah* in front of the Congregation is such an honor that it is also a moment of spiritual ascent.

The first *Aliyah* is given to a *Kohayn*, the second to a *Levi* and the third and all subsequent *Aliyot* to *Yisraelim*. This order accords honor to the priests who performed the service in the Temple and also to the *Levites* who supervised the maintenance of the ancient Temple and its sacred rituals. It also forestalls any rivalry that might arise from everyone clamoring for the first *Aliyah*.

ORDER OF THE *TORAH* SERVICE
("Removal of the *Torah* from the *Aron*")

The service continues with a series of introductory verses celebrating the greatness and majesty of G-d and expressing our desire for Jerusalem to be rebuilt. When the *Aron* is opened, we rise and declare the invincibility of G-d's word.

AV HARACHAMIM
("Father of Compassion")

A 390 BC 277 B 249 M 250 L —

Chazan and Cong. recite or sing in unison.
Av harachamim, haytivah virtzoncha, et tziyon.

Tivneh chomot Yerushalayim.
Ki v'cha l'vad batach-nu,
melech El ram v'nisah, Adon olamim.

THE *ARON* IS OPENED.

VAYHEE BINSOAH

("When the *Aron* would travel")

A 390   BC 277   B 249   M 250   L 117

This prayer acknowledges our gratitude for having received the *Torah* and its blessings, and recalls the way the *Aron* was carried in front of the procession in the Sinai Desert during Biblical times.

Chazan *and Cong. sing in unison.*

Vayhee binsoah ha-aron, vayomer Moshe.
Kumah Adonai, v'yafutzu oyvechah,
v'yanusu m'sanecha mi-panecha.
Ki mi-tziyon taytzeh Torah,
u'dvar Adonai mi-Yerushalayim.
Baruch she-natan, Torah, Torah,
l'amo Yisrael bikdushato.

✌ ADONAI, ADONAI ✌

("The Thirteen Attributes of Mercy")

A 392   BC 277   B 249   M 251   L 117

We recite The Thirteen Attributes of Mercy, celebrating G-d's compassion and kindness.

Recited three times (except on Shabbat, *when it is often omitted).*

Chazan *and Cong. recite aloud or sing in unison.*

Adonai, Adonai, El, Rachum, v'Chanun,
Erech apayim, v'Rav chesed, v'Emet,
Notsayr chesed la-alafim, Noseh avon, va-Fesha,
v'Chata-ah, v'Nakeh.

At the time of the opening of the *Aron*, when G-d's mercy is upon us, we recite a moving prayer, *Ribono Shel Olam*

ᔥ *The Thirteen Attributes* ᔧ

 hen Moses prayed to G-d to forgive the Children of Israel's sin of the Golden Calf (Exodus 34:6-7), G-d in response revealed His Thirteen Attributes of Mercy. In the *Talmud* (*Rosh Hashanah* 17b), we read that G-d appeared to Moses as a *Chazan* in a *tallit* and said, "Whenever Israel sins, let them carry out this service before Me [that is, recite the Thirteen Attributes], and I will forgive them."

An explanation

Adonai: He is merciful (to one before he sins).

Adonai: He is merciful (to the sinner who repents).

El: He is powerful.

Rachum: He is compassionate.

V'Chanun: He graciously grants even undeserved favors.

Erech Apayim: He is slow to anger, allowing the sinner time to repent and thus not requiring immediate punishment.

V'rav Chesed: He abounds in lovingkindness and leniency.

V'emet: He abounds in truth and keeps His promises.

Notsair Chesed L'alafim: He maintains lovingkindness to the thousandth generation.

Noseh Avon: He forgives sins that result from temptation.

Vafesha: He forgives sins of rebellion against Him.

V'Chata-ah: He forgives sins committed carelessly or unknowingly.

V'Nakeh: He completely forgives the sinner who returns to Him with sincere repentance.

Thirteen is the sum of the three Hebrew letters making up the word *echad* ("one"). This indicates that although there are thirteen different attributes of G-d's mercy, they add up to one perfect unity. These Divine Attributes are not an attempt to describe G-d, something Judaism shies away from, but rather an attempt to sum up the essence of ethical behavior; we should look to G-d's attributes as our standard for morality.

("Master of the Universe") asking G-d to pardon us and grant us a long life engaged in *Torah*. [Omitted when *Rosh Hashanah* falls on *Shabbat*.]

VA-ANI T'FILATI
("For me, may my prayer")

> **A 392 BC 279 B 251 M 252 L 117**

Recited three times (except on Shabbat).

Chazan *and Cong. recite aloud or sing in unison.*
Va-ani t'filati, l'chah, Adonai, et ratzon,
Elohim, b'rav chesdecha, anayni, b'emet yishecha.

BEH ANA RACHITZ
("In Him I put my trust")

> **A 394 BC 281 B 253 M 254 L 118**

These are the concluding lines of *Brich Sh'may* ("Blessed is the Name"), a prayer written in Aramaic, depicting G-d's mercy, praising Him and extolling His goodness on behalf of the people of Israel. Rabbi Simeon in the 2nd century stated that "when the Torah is removed to be read, the gates of mercy in heaven are opened and the attribute of G-d's love is stirred up"(*Zohar Vayakhayl*).

Chazan *and Cong. recite or sing in unison.*
Beh, beh ana rachitz.
V'lishmay kadishah, kadishah yakirah,
ana aymar tushbe-chan.

Beh ana rachitz, Beh ana rachitz.
V'lishmay kadishah, kadishah yakirah,
ana aymar tushbe-chan.

Yehay rabbah kadamach,
d'tiftach liba-ee b'o-raytah,
v'tashlim misha-lin d'liba-ee,
v'libah d'chal amach, Yisrael,
l'tav ul'chayin, v'lishlam, Amen.

Two Torah *Scrolls are removed, the* Aron *is closed
and the* Chazan *and Congregation responsively chant*
Shema Yisrael ("Hear O Israel") *and* Echad Elohaynu ("Our
G-d is one"). *The third sentence,* Gadlu ("Declare the
greatness"), *is recited by the* Chazan *alone.*

🕉 SHEMA YISRAEL 🕉
("Hear O Israel")

A 394 BC 281 B 253 M 254 L 118

**Shema Yisrael, Adonai Elohaynu, Adonai Echad.
Echad Elohaynu, Gadol Adonaynu,
   Kadosh v'Norah Sh'mo.
Gadlu LaAdonai Eetee, Un'romemah Sh'mo Yachdav.**

We pay homage to the Torah *now as the scrolls are escorted
through the Congregation. While the* Torahs *are carried around
the synagogue to the* Bimah, *the hymn* L'chah Adonai
("To you, G-d") is sung.

L'CHAH ADONAI
("To You, G-d")

A 394 BC 281 B 253 M 255 L 118

Chazan and Cong. sing in unison.

**L'chah Adonai hag'dulah, v'hag'vurah, v'hatiferet,
v'hanaytzach, v'ha-hod, ki chol bashamayim uva-aretz.
L'chah Adonai hamamlachah v'hamitna-seh
l'chol l'rosh. Romemu Adonai Elohaynu, v'hishtachavu
lahadom raglav kadosh hu. Romemu Adonai Elohaynu,
v'hishtachavu l'har kadsho, ki kadosh Adonai Elohaynu.**

🕉 READING OF THE BIBLE PORTION 🕉

Day 1	A 402	BC 287	B 259	M 258	L 119
Day 2	A 402	BC 299	B 529	M 262	L 119

On the first day, the *Torah* reading is from *Genesis* 21:1-
34. In this portion Sarah is remembered by G-d after being
barren. She miraculously gave birth to Isaac at age ninety.

Our sages teach that three women, Sarah, Rachel and
Chanah, all previously barren, were given the blessing of
children on *Rosh Hashanah*. The theme of this reading is an
acknowledgement of G-d's mercy and remembrance, which
is one of the main ideas of *Rosh Hashanah*.

On the second day, the *Torah* Reading is from *Genesis*
22:1-24, in which we read of the *Akayda*, which is when
Abraham was asked by G-d to sacrifice his son Isaac.
Abraham agrees to do so and is stopped by G-d's angel at the
very last minute. This is unquestionably one of the great
events in Jewish history, teaching us the lesson of faith in
G-d and demonstrating the absolute belief in G-d our
forefathers had.

Five men (seven on *Shabbat*) are called upon to recite
blessings in praise of the *Torah* and the Bible is read in a
musical cantillation used only on the High Holidays. It is
customary in many synagogues to give the *Ba-al Tokea* ("the
one who blows the *shofar*") an *Aliyah*.

BLESSINGS OF THE *TORAH*

If given the honor to recite the blessings, the Ba-al Koreh
(one who reads the Torah*) will show you the place where the
reading commences. Take the corner of your* Tallit, *touch the
place where the reading will begin, kiss the* Tzitzit *and recite
aloud the following blessing:*

Day 1	A 398	BC 287	B 259	M 257	L 119
Day 2	A 398	BC 287	B 529	M 257	L 119

Reader of blessings recites.

Barchu et Adonai Ham-vorach.

Cong. responds, Reader of blessings repeats.

Baruch Adonai Ham-vorach l'olam va-ed.

Reader of blessings recites.

**Baruch atah Adonai, Elohaynu melech ha-olam,
asher ba-char banu, mikol ha-amim,
v'na-tan la-nu et torato.**

Baruch atah Adonai, notayn haTorah. *Cong.* Amen.

*At the conclusion of the reading, take the corner of your
Tallit, touch the place where the reading has just ended, kiss
the Tzitzit and recite the following blessing aloud.*

Reader of blessings recites.
**Baruch atah Adonai, Elohaynu melech ha-olam,
asher na-tan lanu torat emet,
v'cha-yay olam nata b'tochaynu.
Baruch atah Adonai, notayn haTorah.** *Cong.* Amen.

At the conclusion of the *Torah* reading from the first
scroll, the Half *Kaddish* is recited and two people are called
to lift and to tie the *Torah*. The one who lifts the *Torah* is
called the *Magbeah* and the one who ties it is called the
Gollel. The purpose of raising the *Torah* is to show that the
Torah is an open book and belongs to all the people. When
the *Torah* is lifted, the Congregation rises and chants:

V'ZOT HATORAH
("This is the *Torah*")

Day 1	A 412	BC 293	B 265	M 265	L 121
Day 2	A 412	BC 303	B 533	M 265	L 121

Cong. recites aloud or sings in unison.
**V'zot hatorah asher sam Moshe,
Lifnay b'nay Yisrael, al pi Adonai, b'yad Moshe.**

("This is the *Torah* that Moses placed before
the children of Israel at the command of G-d.")

The second *Torah* reading is from *Numbers* 29:1-6 and is
the same for both days. It relates the sacrificial service for
Rosh Hashanah and also the New Moon sacrifice, for *Rosh
Hashanah* also is the beginning of a new month.

This *aliyah*, the last one, is called *Maftir* and the person
called upon to recite the blessings will also chant the
Haftarah. Once again, at the conclusion of this reading, the
Torah is lifted and the Congregation rises and recites in
unison, *V'zot HaTorah* ("This is the *Torah*").

☜ **READING FROM THE PROPHETS** ☞
(The *Haftarah*)

Day 1	A 416	BC 295	B 267	M 268	L 122
Day 2	A 416	BC 305	B 535	M 272	L 122

A section from the Prophets, having a connection to the Bible portion, is chanted.

On the first day, the *Haftarah Reading* is from *Samuel* 1:1-2:10, and similar to the *Torah* reading, after being barren for a long time, Chanah is remembered by G-d and gives birth to Samuel. This reading teaches us that sincere prayer can overcome difficulties and obstacles.

On the second day, the *Haftarah* Reading is from *Jeremiah* 31:1-19. G-d promises Jeremiah that the Jews will be redeemed after the Babylonian Exile. The final verse of this *Haftarah* can also be found in the *Mussaf Shemoneh Esray* as part of the section of Remembrances.

After the *Haftarah*, depending on the custom of the synagogue, special prayers may be recited for the government and for the welfare of the State of Israel. Prior to the sounding of the *shofar*, the Rabbi will usually deliver a sermon

If *Rosh Hashanah* falls on the Sabbath, the *shofar* is not blown and both *Torahs* are returned to the *Aron* (see page 54).

☜ **TKIYAT SHOFAR** ☞
("Blowing of the Shofar")

Day 1	A 432	BC 315	B 281	M 281	L 127
Day 2	A 432	BC 315	B 545	M 281	L 127

The importance of the *shofar* blowing on *Rosh Hashanah* is derived from the *Torah*, which calls this day *Yom Teruah* ("A day of blowing"). The sounding of the *shofar* is not only a biblical decree, but *shofar blowing* represents a call to repentance and awakening. The *shofar* is an instrument from ancient times used for many purposes. Besides its use throughout Jewish history in announcing significant events it will be the instrument through which G-d will remember His people at redemption.

The three types of *shofar* blasts are:

TEKIAH — One long clear sound.

SHEVARIM — Three sounds of medium length.

TERUAH — A minimum of nine sounds of short length.

Even though, there are basically only three different types of sounds, the *shofar* blasts are intermingled within a series of other *shofar* blasts in order to satisfy the various rabbinical opinions as to the order of the sounding of the *shofar*. The *shofar* is not sounded when *Rosh Hashanah* falls on the Sabbath.

LAM'NA-TZAY-ACH
("For the Conductor")

Prior to the blowing of the *shofar*, the Congregation rises and recites Psalm 47, *Lam'na-tzay-ach Livnay Korach* ("For the conductor, to the sons of Korach"), seven times. It is an appropriate introduction to this sacred ceremony, for the *shofar* heralds the recognition by all nations of the Kingship of G-d, which is one of the main themes of *Rosh Hashanah*. The Psalm is recited seven times which corresponds to the number of times G-d's name of *Elohim* as the G-d of Justice is mentioned in this Psalm. Hence, *Elohim* is mentioned forty-nine times, alluding to the levels of holiness and purity which we strive to attain.

Day 1	A 432	BC 315	B 281	M 282	L 127
Day 2	A 432	BC 315	B 545	M 282	L 127

Cong. and Ba'al Tokea *recite together seven times.*

Lam'na tzay-ach livnay, Korach Mizmor.
Kal ha-amim tik'u kaf, ha-ri-u Laylohim b'kol rinah.
Ki Adonai elyon norah, melech gadol al kal ha-aretz.
Yadbayr amim tach-taynu, ul'oomim tachat raglaynu.
Yivchar lanu et nachalataynu, et g'on Ya-akov

asher ahayv, Selah.
Alah Elohim biteruah, Adonai b'kol shofar.
Zamru Elohim zamayru, zamru l'malkaynu za-mayru.
Ki Melech kal ha-aretz Elohim, zamru maskil.
Malach Elohim al goyim,
   Elohim yashav al kiseh kadsho.
N'deevay amim ne-esafu, am Elohay Avraham,
   ki laylohim mageenay eretz, m'od na-alah.

MIN HAMAYTZAR
("From the Depths")

Just before reciting the blessings, the *Baal Tokea* ("One who blows the *shofar*") and the Congregation recite the seven verses beginning with *Min Hamaytzar* (From the depths). We call to G-d in distress facing His judgment and hope that He will answer our prayers with mercy. The initials of the next six verses form the Hebrew acrostic, *Kera Satan* ("May Satan be cut off"), indicating an implied hope that G-d will defend us against the evil inclination.

Day 1 A 434	BC 315	B 281	M 284	L 127
Day 2 A 434	BC 315	B 545	M 284	L 127

Baal Tokea *recites each line. Congregation repeats.*

Min hamaytzar karati Yah, anani vamerchav Yah.
Koli sha-mata, al ta-alem azn'cha, l'rav-chati l'shav-ati.
Rosh d'varcha emet, ool'olam kal mishpat tzidkeh-chah.
Arov avd'cha l'tov, al ya-ash-kuni zaydim.
Sas anochi al imra-techa, k'motzay sha-lal rav.
Tuv ta-am vadaat lam-daynee, ki v'mitz-votecha he-emanti.
Nidvot pi r'tzeh na, Adonai, umishpa-techa lamdaynee.

The *Baal Tokea* is poised, ready to recite the blessings of the *shofar*. In order to help maintain the total concentration required, he will be assisted by the *Baal Makrey*, who will call out the names of the *shofar* sounds. The Congregation stands in awe and silence as they did on Mount Sinai, awaiting the piercing sounds that herald the call of the return to G-d.

ᕗ *The Blowing of the Shofar* ᕤ

n the tenth century Saadiah Gaon enumerated ten different reasons for the blowing of the *shofar*:

1. *Rosh Hashanah* is the anniversary of the creation of the universe and the beginning of G-d's reign. Just like we sound trumpets in the presence of a king so is the *shofar* blown for our King. "With trumpets and the sound of the *shofar* shout before the King, the Lord" (*Psalms* 98:6).

2. Since *Rosh Hashanah* initiates the Ten Days of Penitence the *shofar* is sounded to warn us, "Whoever desires to repent let him do so now, if not, let him reproach himself."

3. When the *Torah* was given at Sinai, the *shofar* was blown: "And the trumpet grew louder and louder" (Exodus 19:19). The *shofar*, therefore, reminds us of our sacred commitment to accept the *Torah* and keep its commandments.

4. The *shofar* reminds us of the warnings and exhortations of the Prophets who called the Jews to repent: "Shall a *shofar* be blown in a city and the people not tremble? Shall evil befall a city and the Lord hath not done it?" (Amos 3:6). We too are reminded to take to heart the warnings of the *shofar.*

5. The *shofar* reminds us of the battle cries of our enemies while they destroyed our holy Temple. When we hear the shofar we are reminded to ask G-d to rebuild the Temple.

6. We are reminded by the *shofar* (which is a ram's horn) of the *Akaydah*, ("the Binding of Isaac") when Abraham sacrificed a ram instead of his son Isaac. We are called upon to emulate the spirit of self-sacrifice shown by Abraham.

7. The *shofar* inspires us with awe and reverence.

8. The *shofar* reminds us of the Day of Judgment.

9. The *shofar* inspires us with hope for the restoration of Israel. "And it shall come to pass on that day that a great *shofar* shall be blown and they shall come who were lost in the land of Assyria and worship the Lord in the holy mountain at Jerusalem" (Isaiah 27:13).

10. The *shofar* strengthens our belief in the resurrection of the dead and the immortality of the soul.

BLESSINGS OF THE SHOFAR

The *Baal Tokea* cognizant of the great importance of the moment intones the blessing, "Blessed art Thou, O Lord our G-d, King of the Universe, who hast sanctified us by Your commandments and has commanded us to hear the sound of the *shofar.*" This is followed by the blessing *Sheh-hecheyanu* thanking G-d for allowing us to live and keep His commandments. The Congregation listens intently to the blessings and responds *Amen.*

Day 1	A 436	BC 317	B 283	M 285	L 127
Day 2	A 436	BC 317	B 547	M 285	L 127

Baal Tokea *recites alone.*

Baruch Atah Adonai, Elohaynu Melech Ha-olam, Asher Kidshanu B'mitzvotav, V'tzeevanu Lishmoa Kol Shofar. *Cong. responds Amen.*

Baruch Atah Adonai, Elohaynu Melech Ha-olam, Sheh-hecheyanu, V'keeyamanu, V'higiyanu, Lazman Hazeh. *Cong. responds Amen.*

It should be noted that in the first blessing, we do not say "and hast commanded us to blow the *shofar,*" but "and has commanded us to hear the sound of the *shofar.*" We fulfill the Divine command only when we hear the sound of the *shofar*, when we take to heart the message it proclaims — to serve G-d with all our hearts and to fulfill all His commandments.

The total number of *shofar* blasts to be sounded on *Rosh Hashanah* will be one hundred. The following three groups of *shofar* sounds will form the first part of the *shofar* blowing (Thirty in total). The balance (seventy sounds) will be blown during the *Chazan*'s repetition of the *Shemoneh Esray* and at the end of the *Mussaf Service.* From the moment the first blessing of the *shofar* is recited up to the last of the *shofar* blasts it is forbidden to talk.

TEKIAH, SHEVARIM – TERUAH, TEKIAH,
TEKIAH, SHEVARIM – TERUAH, TEKIAH,
TEKIAH, SHEVARIM – TERUAH, TEKIAH,

TEKIAH, SHEVARIM, TEKIAH,
TEKIAH, SHEVARIM, TEKIAH,
TEKIAH, SHEVARIM, TEKIAH,

TEKIAH, TERUAH, TEKIAH,
TEKIAH, TERUAH, TEKIAH,
TEKIAH, TERUAH, TEKIAH GEDOLAH,

In between each of the three groups of *shofar* sounds is a short supplication, *Y'hee Ratzon* ("May it be Your will"). These mystical pleas are not to be recited, since they would interrupt the sounds of the *shofar*. They may, however, be scanned with our eyes.

ASHRAY HA-AM
(Concluding Verses)

At this point, three verses from Psalm 89 are recited. They offer final praises to G-d and to the Nation of Israel who have now heard the sound of the *shofar* and understand their meaning.

Day 1	A 438	BC 319	B 285	M 286	L 128
Day 2	A 438	BC 319	B 549	M 286	L 128

Baal Tokea *recites each line, Cong. repeats.*

**Ashray ha-am yod'ay teruah, Adonai,
b'or panecha y'ha-lay-chun.
B'shimcha y'gi-lun kal hayom, uv'tzid-katcha yarumu.
Ki tiferet uzamo atah, uvirtzoncha tarum karnaynu.**

✍ THE TORAHS ARE RETURNED TO THE *ARON* ✍

After sounding the *shofar*, Psalm 145 (*Ashray*) is recited and the *Torah* scrolls are returned to the *Aron*. A series of special supplications are recited, concluding with the hope that

Israel should be worthy of being host to G-d's holiness and asking that G-d renew the days of old.

The Torah *scrolls are lifted and escorted back to the* Aron.
They are once again carried throughout the Congregation and during this procession, the following hymns praising the glory of G-d are chanted.

Y'HALELU
("Let them praise")

Chazan *recites.*

Y'halelu et shaym, Adonai, ki nisgav sh'mo l'vado.

Cong. responds.

Day 1	A 440	BC 321	B 287	M 289	L 129
Day 2	A 440	BC 321	B 551	M 289	L 129

Hodo al eretz, v'shamayim, vayah-rem keren l'amo, tehilah l'chol chasidav, livnay Yisrael am k'rovo, Halleluyah.

L'DAVID MIZMOR
("A Psalm of David")

A 442	BC 323	B 289	M 289	L —

When *Rosh Hashanah* falls on a weekday, Psalm 24, *L'David Mizmor* ("To David, a Psalm") is recited. Please refer to your *Machzor* for this prayer. When *Rosh Hashanah* occurs on *Shabbat, Mizmor L'David* ("A Psalm to David") is chanted by the *Chazan* and Congregation. In many synagogues, this Psalm is sung together.

The Aron *is opened, the* Torah *scrolls are returned to the* Aron Hakodesh *and after the recital of a few verses, the following beautiful hymn is sung by the* Chazan *and Congregation.*

ETZ CHAYIM HIH
("A tree of life for those [who grasp it]")

Day 1	A 444	BC 323	B 288	M 292	L —
Day 2	A 444	BC 323	B 553	M 292	L —

Etz chayim hih, lamachazikim bah,

v'tomcheha m'ushar.
Dira-che-ha, darchay no-am,
v'chal netivoteh-hah shalom.

Hashivaynu Adonai,
aylechah v'na-shu-vah,
chadaysh yamaynu k'kedem.

THE ARON *IS CLOSED*

The *Ba-al Mussaf* ("Cantor for the Additional Service") stands in his place, concentrating intently on his mission, preparing himself to lead the Congregation in the *Mussaf.*

Mussaf
The Additional Service

Mussaf is the additional service recited on all Sabbaths, New Moons and Festivals. The name *Mussaf* means "additional" and it commemorates as well as replaces the extra sacrifices that were offered on special days in our ancient Temple. These additions to the daily Temple Service symbolized the added holiness of the Sabbath or Festival.

The main part of the *Mussaf* Service of *Rosh Hashanah* consists of the *Shemoneh Esray* recited quietly by the Congregation and then the *Chazan*'s repetition, which includes additional *Shofar* blasts and some of the most important prayers of the day.

🕊 HINENI 🕊
(The *Chazan*'s Prayer)

Day 1	A 444	BC 325	B 291	M 293	L 129
Day 2	A 444	BC 325	B 555	M 293	L 129

In this introductory prayer prior to the *Mussaf* Service the *Chazan* expresses his unworthiness to represent the Congregation before G-d, yet beseeches G-d to accept his prayers as well as the prayers of the Congregation.

✌ HALF KADDISH ☞

In this beautiful and ancient prayer we ask that G-d's name be exalted throughout the world. It is chanted by the *Chazan* in an ancient melody The most important part is the Congregational response, *Amen, Y'hay sh'may rabbah m'varach* . . . ("May His great name be blessed forever and ever"), which should be recited aloud.

Day 1	A 446	BC 327	B 293	M 295	L 130
Day 2	A 446	BC 327	B 557	M 295	L 130

Chazan *recites:*

Yitgadal, v'yitkadash, sh'may rabbah. *Cong. responds* Amen.
B'almah di-v'ra chirutay, v'yamlich malchutay,
b'chayaychon uv'yomaychon, u'v'chayay d'chol
bayt Yisrael, ba-agalah uvizman kareev,
v'imru, Amen. *Cong. responds* Amen.

Chazan *and Cong. recite together:* **Y'hay sh'may rabbah**
m'varach, l'alam ul'almay almayah.

Yitbarach, v'yishtabach, v'yit-pa-ar, v'yit-romam,
v'yit-naseh, v'yit-hadar, v'yit-aleh, v'yit-halal,
sh'may d'kudshah, B'rich Hu. *Cong. responds* B'rich Hu.

L'aylah, l'aylah, mikol birchatah v'shiratah,
tushb'chatah, v'ne-chematah, da-amiran b'almah,
v'imru, Amen. *Cong. responds* Amen.

✌ SHEMONEH ESRAY ☞
(Silent Devotion)

Day 1	A 448	BC 327	B 293	M 296	L 130
Day 2	A 448	BC 327	B 557	M 528	L 130

The *Shemoneh Esray* or *Amida* is the highlight of the *Mussaf* Service, and like all the daily silent devotional prayers it is divided into three sections.

Praise—In the first three blessings of the Silent Devotion, we recognize, describe and praise the glory of G-d.

Petition—The middle blessing expresses the sanctity of the day. This blessing also asks G-d to restore the Holy Temple Service.

Thanksgiving—The final three blessings express our gratitude to G-d and include a prayer for peace as well as a personal prayer asking G-d to protect us.

Both the opening section of the Silent Devotion (praise of G-d) and the closing section (our expression of thanksgiving) are exactly the same as in the other services. But in the middle section (petition) there is an addition of three blessings. Each of these blessings contains an introductory paragraph, ten biblical verses, a supplication and a concluding blessing. They are grouped under the following headings.

Malchuyot ("Kingship")—In this blessing we affirm our belief that we are G-d's chosen people and that He is our King, our G-d, the One and Only. We dedicate *Rosh Hashanah* to proclaiming that G-d, the King of Kings, rules the entire universe and will one day be exalted over the universe in His splendor and grandeur.

Zichronot ("Remembrances")—We acknowledge in this blessing that G-d remembers everything and that nothing can be hidden from His eyes. We declare our awareness that *Rosh Hashanah* is a time of remembrance for every spirit and soul, a time for all mortals to be judged. But before we are judged, we remind G-d of the compassion he showed towards our ancestors, Noach, Abraham, Isaac and Jacob. We ask G-d to remember the oath He made to Abraham at the *Akayda*, when he swore to bless Abraham and his offspring. We ask only that G-d suppress His anger and treat us with mercy.

Shofarot ("*Shofar* Blasts")—The *shofar* was first mentioned in the *Torah* at the extraordinary revelation at Mount Sinai when G-d gave Moses the Ten Commandments. "And it came to pass . . . there were thunderbolts and flashes

ᔌ *Reciting the Silent Devotion* ᔎ

his prayer is called either the *Amida* ("standing") or the *Shemoneh Esray* ("eighteen"). There is evidence in the *Torah* that the blessings in the *Shemoneh Esray* date back to Abraham, Issac and Jacob, although the final form was arranged in Babylonia by the Rabbis of the Great Assembly.

At all times keep in mind that prayer is communication with G-d. Rabbi Eliezer ben Hyrcanus, a prominent 1st-century scholar, reminded his students: "When you pray, know before Whom you are standing."

The Rabbis prescribed a strict etiquette for how to stand before G-d when we pray:

1. Before praying, take three steps backwards (starting with your left foot) and then three steps forward (the way one would approach a king). Then remain absolutely still with both feet together throughout the prayer (as a sign of respect and also to signify your earnest desire to speak to G-d).

2. Recite the prayer softly, articulating each word so that you hear yourself.

3. In the opening prayer, bend knees at the word *Baruch* ("Blessed"), then bow at the word *Attah* ("You"), straightening back up at the name of G-d. Do the same at the conclusion of the first blessing. The same procedure is repeated at the end of the *Shemoneh Esray*, at *Modim* ("We thank You"), bowing at the beginning and end of the blessing.

4. When you recite the words "He Who makes peace," found in the next-to-last paragraph of the *Shemoneh Esray*, take three steps backwards, beginning with your left foot. Then bow three times, once to the left, once to the right, then forward. This symbolizes your departure from G-d's throne. Finally, take three steps forward and remain in place for a few seconds after the *Shemoneh Esray*.

of lightning . . . and an exceeedingly loud *shofar* blast"
(*Exodus* 19:16).

This blessing is introduced with a moving recounting of
the events at Sinai, the world trembling as G-d revealed
Himself and taught the Jews the *Torah* and *mitzvot*. And it
was with the sound of the *shofar* on that day that these
events transpired: "While the *shofar* blast grew louder,
Moshe spoke and G-d answered him" (*Exodus* 19:19), "And
all the people saw the voices and the flames and the call of
the shofar" (*Exodus* 20:15). The narrative goes on to note
other dramatic times in Jewish history that the *shofar* has
been sounded. We end with a request that the *shofar* will be
the vehicle to announce our future redemption, when all the
Jews dispersed throughout the world will be gathered
together in Jerusalem and the Temple will be rebuilt.

Since the *Mussaf Amida* is the most important *Shemoneh
Esray* of the day, it should be recited with particular concentration and devotion. We have included no transliteration
since the *Shemoneh Esray* is recited quietly. *For further
explanation of* Shemoneh Esray, *see pages* 9 and 10.

❦ CHAZARAT HASHATZ ❦
("*Chazan*'s Repetition")

Day 1	A 470	BC 349	B 315	M 330	L 139
Day 2	A 536	BC 359	B 579	M 560	L 139

The public repetition by the *Chazan* of the *Shemoneh
Esray* (or *Amida*) is an important part of the service,
especially on the High Holidays. Several liturgical poems
(*piyutim*) expressing the theme of the day have been inserted
to underline the significance of the Days of Awe. These
beautiful compositions filled with allegory and metaphor
were composed by medieval poets and by *Chazanim.* Many
were written by Meshullam ben Kalonymos in the 10th
century and are usually arranged in some form of alphabetical
order. The names of the authors of the *piyutim* can
sometimes be identified within the verse's arrangement.

The *Chazan*'s repetition is communal prayer, and several of the most important prayers of *Rosh Hashanah* are included. At various times the *Aron* is opened, and it is respectful to rise.

In many synagogues, the *Chazan* will sing parts of the repetition and worshippers will join in. We have transliterated some of the prayers frequently sung by the *Chazan* and the Congregation together.

During every *Shemoneh Esray* prayer (including the *Chazan*'s repetition) in the Ten-Day Penitential period, four additional phrases dating back to the Gaonic period (9th-11th century) are inserted in the *Shemoneh Esray*. These phrases express the theme of repentance, with the continual plea that G-d grant us forgiveness.

ZACHRAYNU L'CHAYIM
("Remember us for life")

The first of the four special High Holiday insertions to *Shemoneh Esray* is located before the blessing of *Magen Avraham* ("Shield of Abraham"). In this prayer we ask G-d to remember us and inscribe us in the Book of Life.

Day 1	A 472	BC 351	B 317	M 331	L 140
Day 2	A 536	BC 359	B 579	M 560	L 140

Cong. recites, Chazan *repeats, or sung in unison.*

Zachraynu l'chayim, melech chafetz bachayim, v'chatvaynu b'sefer hachayim, l'ma-ancha Elohim chayim.

M'CHALKAYL CHAYIM
("Sustainer of the living")

The above blessing is followed with a prayer praising G-d's strength and describing how He sustains us.

Day 1	A 472	BC 351	B 317	M 331	L 140
Day 2	A 536	BC 359	B 579	M 561	L 141

Chazan *recites, or sung with Cong.*

Atah gibor l'olam Adonai,

m'chayay maytim atah, rav l'hoshee-ah.

M'chalkayl chayim b'chesed,
m'chayay maytim b'rachamim rabim.
So-mech noflim, v'rofeh cholim,
umatir asurim, u'm'kayem emunato,
leey'shaynay ahfar.
Mi chamochah ba-al g'vurot, umi domeh lach,
melech maymit u'mchayeh,
umatzmi-ach yeshuah.

MI CHAMOCHAH
("Who is like You")

This is the second of the four special High Holiday phrases recited in the Silent Devotion. It is said just prior to the blessing of *M'chayay Hamaytim* ("Resuscitator of the dead").

Day 1	A 476	BC 353	B 319	M 332	L 141
Day 2	A 536	BC 359	B 579	M 561	L 142

Cong. recites, Chazan *repeats, or sung in unison.*

Mi chamocha av harachamim,
zocher yetzurav l'chayim b'rachamim.

SOME CONGREGATIONS WILL
NOW RECITE VARIOUS *PIYUTIM.*

Some of the more significant prayers in the Chazan's *repetition:*

FOR SECOND DAY OF *ROSH HASHANAH*, SEE PAGE 65.

❧ FIRST DAY OF ROSH HASHANAH ☙
MELECH ELYON
("The Supreme King")

This *piyut* is an affirmation of G-d's boundless majesty and infinite power. It is He Who is dependable—a mortal leader invariably perishes, whereas G-d's might is everlasting. This *piyut* contains no requests from us, it is simply a celebratory poem in honor of the glory of G-d.

Each sentence ends with the statement *La-aday Ad Yimloch Melech Elyon* ("Forever shall He reign, the Supreme King"). This hymn is recited in the *Mussaf* Service the first day, and a somewhat similar version is recited in the *Shacharit* Service for the second day.

| A 478 | BC 355 | B 321 | M 333 | L 142 |

THE *ARON* IS OPENED.

The first four stanzas have been transliterated, since only these are usually sung aloud.

Chazan *recites, Cong. repeats.*

**Uv'chayn vay'hee
veeshu-roon melech, Melech Elyon.**

Cong. recites, Chazan repeats.

**El dar bamarom,
adir bamarom,
ometz yado tarom,
    La-aday Ad Yimloch, Melech Elyon.**

**Gibor l'hakim,
gozer umay-kim,
goleh amukim,
    La-aday Ad Yimloch, Melech Elyon.**

**Ham'da-bayr bitz'dakah,
ha-lo-vaysh tz'dakah,
ha-ma-azin tz'a-kah,
    La-aday Ad Yimloch, Melech Elyon.**

**Zochayr tzurim,
zakot y'tzurim,
zo-aym tzarim,
    La-aday Ad Yimloch, Melech Elyon.**

Please consult your machzor *for the balance of the poem.*

THE *ARON* IS CLOSED.

ON THE FIRST DAY, CONTINUE WITH
UNETANEH TOKEF ON PAGE 67.

✣ SECOND DAY OF ROSH HASHANAH ✣
L'EL ORECH DIN
("To G-d in Judgment")

This alphabetically arranged *piyut* praises the attributes of G-d as He sits in judgment and is filled with forgiveness, compassion and mercy. Every first half-line ends with the words *B'yom Din* ("On the day of judgment"); the other half-line ends with the word *Badin* ("With judgment"). The poem is chanted with intense feeling, so that we can loudly and communally proclaim each of G-d's attributes.

THE *ARON* IS OPENED.

A 538   BC 261   B 581   M 561   L 142

Chazan *recites,* Cong. *repeats.*
Uv'chayn l'chah hakol yachtiru, L'el orech din.

Cong. *recites,* Chazan *repeats.*

L'vochen l'vavot,	b'yom din,
l'goleh amukot,	badin.
L'dovayr maysharim,	b'yom din,
l'hogeh day-ot,	badin.
L'vatik v'oseh chesed,	b'yom din,
l'zochayr b'rito,	badin.
L'chomayl ma-asav,	b'yom din,
l'ta-hayr cho-sav,	badin.
L'yoday-a machshavot,	b'yom din,
l'cho-vaysh ka-aso,	badin.
L'lovaysh tz'dakot,	b'yom din,
l'mochayl avonot,	badin.
L'norah t'hilot,	b'yom din,
l'solayach la-amusav,	badin.
L'oneh l'kor'av,	b'yom din,
l'fo-ayl rachamav,	badin.
L'tzofeh nistarot,	b'yom din,

৶ *Unetaneh Tokef* ৶

ne of the most stirring compositions recited on *Rosh Hashanah* is the *Unetaneh Tokef* prayer, traditionally attributed to Rabbi Amnon of Mainz, Germany, who lived *circa* one thousand years ago. The seriousness and cadence of this *piyut* leaves a deep impression on worshippers because this prayer describes our transience. The story behind *Unetaneh Tokef*: One day the local bishop of Mainz summoned Rabbi Amnon, a respected and learned man, to his court and offered him a ministerial post on the condition that he convert to Christianity. Rabbi Amnon, of course, refused. Day after day the bishop insisted that Rabbi Amnon convert, but without success. Finally, one day Rabbi Amnon asked the bishop for three days to consider his offer.

As soon as Rabbi Amnon returned home, he was distraught at having given any impression that he would even consider betraying G-d. For three days he could neither eat nor sleep, and he prayed to be forgiven for his sin. The deadline passed but he stayed home and did not return to the bishop, who sent messenger after messenger to fetch him. The Rabbi refused to respond and at last was forcibly brought before the bishop. When asked why he had balked, Rabbi Amnon replied, "I should have my tongue cut out for having not immediately refused." The bishop angrily had the Rabbi's hands and feet cut off and then sent him home. A few days later, on *Rosh Hashanah*, Rabbi Amnon, bleeding and suffering, asked to be carried to the synagogue and placed in front of the *Aron*. He wished to say the *Kedushah*, to sanctify G-d's name publicly and declare his unequivocal faith in G-d's sovereignty. With his dying breath, he recited *Unetaneh Tokef*.

Three days later Rabbi Amnon appeared in a dream to Rabbi Kalonymos ben Meshullam, a scholar and poet, and taught him the text of *Unetaneh Tokef*. Rabbi Amnon asked that he send it to all of Jewry and that it be inserted into the *Rosh Hashanah* liturgy. Rabbi Amnon's wish was carried out and soon it was also included in the *Yom Kippur* liturgy.

l'koneh avadav,   badin.

L'rachem amo,   b'yom din,
  l'shomayr ohavav,   badin.

L'tomaych t'mimav,   b'yom din.

THE *ARON* IS CLOSED.

THE SERVICE CONTINUES HERE FOR BOTH DAYS.

THE *ARON* IS OPENED.

৯৮ U'NETANEH TOKEF ৡ

("Let us proclaim")

We continue with this extraordinarily moving *piyut.* (*For explanation and summary of* Unetaneh Tokef, *please refer to pages 66 and 68.*)

Day 1 A 480 BC 361 B 325 M 337 L 144	
Day 2 A 538 BC 361 B 583 M 564 L 144	

Chazan *recites,* Cong. *repeats.*

Uv'chayn ul'chah ta-aleh kedushah,
ki atah Elohaynu melech, mochayl v'solay-ach.

Cong. *and* Chazan *recite together.*

U'netaneh tokef, kedushat hayom,
ki hu norah v'ayom, uvo tinaseh malchutechah,
v'yikon b'chesed kis-echah, v'tayshayv alav b'emet.
Emet ki atah hu dayan, umochiach, v'yoday-a va-ed,
v'chotayv v'chotaym, v'sofayr umoneh, v'tizkor
kol hanishkachot. V'tiftach et sefer hazichronot,
umay-aylav yikareh, v'chotam yad kol adam bo.

Uvashofar gadol yitaka, v'kol d'mama dakah yishama.
Umalachim yaychafayzun, v'cheel ur'adah yochayzun,
v'yomru hineh yom hadin. Lifkod al tz'vah
marom badin, ki lo yizku v'aynechah badin.
V'chol ba-ay olam, ya-avrun l'fanechah, kivnay maron.

K'vakarat roeh edro, maavir tzono tachat shivto,
ken ta-avir, v'tispor v'timneh, v'tifkod nefesh kol chai,

✍ *Unetaneh Tokef Summarized* ✒

his moving prayer is divided into three parts. The first describes the scene in heaven on the Day of Judgment: G-d on His Throne of Judgment, both the Judge and the Witness. He knows all and remembers the forgotten. The Book of Chronicles reads itself to G-d and reveals every person's deeds. Who can deny such a record? Each individual passes in judgment before G-d, a heavenly Shepherd counting His flock, one by one, as our destiny is determined.

The second part of *Unetaneh Tokef* dramatically expresses how profoundly uncertain life is. It reads "On *Rosh Hashanah* it is inscribed and on *Yom Kippur* it is sealed . . . How many will pass on and how many will be born, who shall live and who shall die . . ." All of us are sobered by these thoughts, as we are all subject to the divine hand of G-d. Even the method of punishment or reward is determined by the judgment to be rendered on *Rosh Hashanah* and sealed on *Yom Kippur*: who will enjoy tranquility and who will suffer, who will become impoverished and who will be enriched. But although our fate is decided on this day, the decree can be averted. No matter how sinful we have been, we can still be redeemed, through repentance, prayer and charity, which avert the stern decree.

The third part of the prayer proclaims that G-d does not desire the death of the sinner, G-d awaits repentance until the day of one's death. Our origin is dust and to dust we shall return. We are but a passing shade, a blowing wind and a fleeting dream, but G-d is the King and the living and enduring G-d. We therefore ask G-d to consider our lowliness, decide that our sins are insignificant and grant us complete atonement.

v'tachtoch kitzvah l'chol b'riyotechah,
v'tichtov et g'zar dinam.

Chazan *repeats the final few verses.*

B'ROSH HASHANAH YIKATAY-VUN

("On *Rosh Hashanah* will be inscribed")

Day 1	A 482	BC 361	B 325	M 339	L 144
Day 2	A 540	BC 361	B 583	M 565	L 144

Cong. and Chazan *recite together, although in some synagogues, the* Chazan *recites alone and Cong. follows along.*

B'rosh Hashanah yikatay-vun,
u'vyom Tzom Kippur yay-cha-taymun,
K ahmah ya-avrun, v'chamah yiba-ray-un,

mi yichyeh,	umi yamut,
mi v'kitzo,	umi lo v'kitzo,
mi vamayim,	umi va-esh,
mi vacherev,	umi vachayah,
mi vara-av,	umi vatzamah,
mi va-ra-ash,	umi vamagayfah,
mi vachanikah,	umi vaskilah,
mi yanu-ach,	umi yanu-ah,
mi yishakayt,	umi yitarayf,
mi yishalayv,	umi yityasar,
mi yay-ani,	umi yay-ashayr,
mi yishafayl,	umi yaroom.

Cong. recites loudly, Chazan *repeats.*

U-T'shuvah, U-T'filah, U-Tz'dakah
Mah-avirin Et Ro-ah Hag'zayrah.

("But Repentance, Prayer, and Charity
avert the severity of the decree.")

In some *machzorim*, the words fasting, voice and money are written above repentance, prayer and charity, to show the methods by which one can practice these virtues. The ordeal of fasting leads to repentance, the voice is the route to soul-stirring prayer and the contribution of money to a worthwhile cause is an act of charity.

KI K'SHIMCHA
("For as is Your Name")

Day 1	A 484	BC 363	B 327	M 340	L 144
Day 2	A 540	BC 363	B 585	M 566	L 144

Cong. and Chazan recite together.

Ki k'shimcha kayn t'hilatecha,
kasheh lich-os, v'no-ach lirtzot;
ki lo tachpotz b'mot hamayt,
ki im b'shuvo midarko v'chaya.
V'ad yom moto t'chakeh lo,
im yashuv miyad t'kablo.
Emet, ki atah hu yotzram,
v'atah yoday-ah yitzram, ki haym basar vadam.
Adam, y'sodo may-ahfar, v'sofo l'ahfar.
B'nafsho yavee lachmo;
mashul k'cheres hanishbar, k'chatzir yavaysh,
uch'tzitz novayl, uch'tzayl ovayr,
uch'anan kalah, uch'ru-ach noshavet,
uch'avak poray-ach, v'cha-chalom ya-uf.

Chazan repeats final few verses.
Cong. recites loudly, Chazan repeats.
V'atah Hu Melech, El Chai V'kayam.
("But You are the King, the living and eternal G-d.")

THE *ARON* IS CLOSED.

AYN KITZVAH
("There is no limit")

The Children of Israel join with the angels to praise G-d, in the most important part of the repetition. Prior to the *Kedushah* is the poetic introductory prayer, *Ayn Kitzvah* ("There is no limit"), which compares the transience of humans with the permanence of G-d.

Day 1	A 484	BC 363	B 327	M 341	L 145
Day 2	A 542	BC 363	B 585	M 567	L 145

Cong. recites, Chazan repeats.

Ayn kitzvah lishnotecha,

v'ayn kaytz l'orech yamecha,
v'ayn l'sha-ayr mark'vot k'vodecha,
v'ayn l'faraysh ayloom sh'mecha.
Shimcha na-eh l'chah, v'atah na-eh lishmechah,
ush'maynu karata vishmechah.

Aseh l'ma-an sh'mecha,
v'kadaysh et shimchah,
al makdeeshay sh'mechah.
Ba-avoor k'vod shimcha,
hana-aratz v'hanikdash,
k'sod siyach sarfay kodesh,
hamakdishim shimcha bakodesh,
daray ma-alah im daray matah. . . .

❧ MUSSAF KEDUSHAH ❧
(Sanctification of G-d's Name)

The actual recital of the *Kedushah* begins here. During the *Kedushah* it is customary to keep one's feet together and then rise on one's toes three times at the recital of *Kadosh, Kadosh, Kadosh,* and one time at the recital of *Baruch K'vod Adonai* and *Yimloch Adonai.* In this way we rise as angels toward Heaven, as in *Isaiah* 6:2: "Above him stood the angels and with two [wings they] did fly."

Day 1	A 486	BC 363	B 327	M 342	L 145
Day 2	A 542	BC 363	B 585	M 568	L 145

Cong recites, Chazan repeats.
Kakatoov al yad n'vee-echa, v'karah zeh el zeh v'amar.

Cong. and Chazan together. During the first three words we rise on our toes.
Kadosh, Kadosh, Kadosh, Adonai Tz'va-ot, Meloh Chol Ha-aretz K'vodo.

Cong. recites, Chazan repeats. During the word K'vodo *we rise on our toes.*
K'vodo maleh olam, m'shartav sho-alim zeh lazeh, ayeh m'kom k'vodo, l'umatam baruch yomayroo.

Cong. and Chazan together. During the word Baruch *we rise on our toes.*
Baruch K'vod Adonai Mimkomo.

Cong. recites, Chazan repeats.

**Mimkomo hu yifen b'rachmim,
v'yachon am ham'yachadim sh'mo,
erev vavoker, b'chol yom tamid,
pa-amayim b'ahavah shema omrim.**

Cong. and Chazan together.

Shema Yisrael, Adonai Elohaynu, Adonai Echad.

Cong. recites, Chazan repeats.

**Hu Elohaynu, Hu Avinu, Hu Malkaynu, Hu Mo-shee-aynu.
V'hu yashmee-aynu b'rachamav shaynit l'aynay kol chai.
Lihyot lachem lay-lohim.
Ani Adonai Elohaychem.**

Cong. and Chazan together.

**Adir adeeraynu, Adonai adonaynu,
mah adir shimcha b'chol ha-aretz,
v'hayah Adonai l'melech al kol ha-aretz,
bayom ha-hu yihyeh Adonai echad, ush'mo echad.**

Cong. recites, Chazan repeats.

Uv'divray kad-sh'cha katoov laymor.

Cong. and Chazan together. During the word Yimloch *we rise on our toes.*

***Yimloch Adonai L'olam, Elohayich Tziyon,
L'dor Vador, Halleluyah.***

PRAYERS ARE RECITED BY THE *CHAZAN*
BEFORE CONTINUING WITH THE FOLLOWING:

V'CHOL MA-AMINIM
("And all believe")

This poem is an alphabetically arranged description of how completely we believe in G-d and His consistent fairness toward us. We praise His power, His mercy and His judgment.

THE *ARON* IS OPENED.

| Day 1 | A 490 | BC 367 | B 331 | M 345 | L 145 |
| Day 2 | A 546 | BC 367 | B 589 | M 572 | L 145 |

Only the first four verses have been transliterated since usually only these are sung aloud.

Chazan *recites, Cong. repeats.*

Ha-ochayz b'yad midat mishpat.

Cong recites, Chazan *repeats.*

**V'chol Ma-aminim she-hu El emunah,
habochayn uvodayk, ginzay nistarot.**

**V'chol Ma-aminim she-hu bochayn k'layot,
hago-el mi-mavet, ufodeh mi-shachat.**

**V'chol Ma-aminim she-hu go-ayl chazak,
hadan y'chidi, l'va-ay olam.**

**V'chol Ma-aminim she-hu dayan emet,
heh-ha-gooy, b'eh-yeh asher eh-yeh.**

Please consult your machzor *for the balance of the poem.*

THE *ARON* IS CLOSED.

ADDITIONAL PRAYERS WILL NOW BE RECITED BY
THE *CHAZAN* BEFORE HE CONTINUES WITH *ALAYNU.*

ALAYNU

("It is our duty")

The insertion of *Alaynu* at this point is to introduce the first of the three concepts of the *Rosh Hashanah Shemoneh Esray—Malchuyot* ("Kingship"). We acknowledge that G-d is the Supreme Being and it is incumbent upon us to praise Him, the Ruler of the entire universe. We then express our gratitude to Him for not making us like the other nations of the world.

During *Alaynu,* the *Chazan* kneels to the floor as a commemoration of the kneeling that took place during the service in the days that our Holy Temple stood. The *Chazan* sings *Alaynu* in the traditional melody and the Congregation follows softly.

THE *ARON* IS OPENED.

Day 1	A 500	BC 377	B 341	M 355	L 149
Day 2	A 554	BC 377	B 599	M 581	L 149

**Alaynu l'shabayach la-adon hakol,
latayt g'dula l'yotzayr b'raysheet.**

🖘 The Meaning of the Shofar 🖙

s the great 12th-century scholar Maimonides said, the *shofar* is sounded as a message to us, "Awake, you who are fast asleep, awake! You slumberers, awake from your deep sleep! Search your deeds and repent; remember your Creator!"

Samson Raphael Hirsch, the brilliant 19th century German scholar wrote, in his brilliant work *Horeb* "In consonance, therefore, with our spiritual thoughts and deeds called into being at *Rosh Hashanah*, the initial *tekiah* signifies introspection and a rising above ourselves; the *teruah* a purification of ourselves; and the final *tekiah* a determination to follow a more righteous future. Thus they correspond to repentance, prayer and charity which our Sages declare are the rich harvest of the Rosh Hashanah day."

Hirsch goes on to say that the tones of the *shofar* evoke in us, "spiritual thinking and acting before G-d. We are summoned by *tekiah*, to appear before G-d our ruler and the ruler of the whole world. We are asked to look inwards and rise above ourselves. With *teruah*, we receive a call to sit in judgment upon ourselves before G-d, the judge. The final *tekiah* resembles our exhausted spirit, as it were, leading us back to a unified, straight and upright life. G-d calls upon us to follow Him along the path He has set for us, he unshackles us from the bonds of the past and strengthens us and raises us— He is both our Father and our Teacher.

Hirsch wrote that since the purpose of the *shofar* is to rouse in us the purely Divine, no artificially constructed instrument may be sounded. That is why, he says, we use the ram's horn which is naturally hollow—a natural musical instrument given life by the breath of man. The ideal shape of the horn is bent to conform with the contrite mood of the day. The ram is the ideal animal to take the horn from since it preserves the noble memory of Abraham's sacrifice.

Shelo asanu k'goyay ha-aratzot,
v'lo samanu k'mishp'chot ha-adama.
Sheh-lo sam chelkaynu kahem,
v'goralaynu k'chol hamonam. *(Chazan kneels)*
Va-anachnu kor'im umishtachavim umodim,
lifnay melech malchay ham'lachim,
Hakadosh Baruch Hu.

THE *ARON* IS CLOSED.

Immediately after reciting *Alaynu,* the *Chazan* makes two appeals to G-d. In the first, *He-yay Im Pifiyot,* he asks that his prayers be received. In the second, *Ocheelah,* he asks that his supplications on behalf of the Congregation be accepted. Following *Ocheelah,* the *Chazan* continues with the second paragraph of *Alaynu, Al kain n'kaveh* ("Therefore, we put our hope"), which extols the mighty and awesome power of G-d among the nations of the world and introduces the rest of the *Malchuyot* section.

MALCHUYOT, ZICHRONOT, SHOFAROT

(Blowing of the Shofar)

Day 1	A 506	BC 381	B 345	M 360	L 150
Day 2	A 558	BC 381	B 603	M 585	L 150

This section of the *Chazan*'s repetition is similar to the Silent Devotion *(please see pages 59 and 61).* But it is in the repetition that the *shofar* is sounded, ten times after each blessing, for a total of thirty blasts. The *Talmud* states: "G-d proclaimed: Recite before Me on the New Year, *Malchuyot* ("Kingship"), *Zichronot* ("Remembrances") and *Shofarot* (*"Shofar* Blasts"). *Malchuyot* verses, in order to proclaim Me King over you, *Zichronot* verses, so that the remembrance of you may come before Me for good; and through what? Through the *shofar*" (*Rosh Hashanah* 34b).

The *Chazan* chants each section in the *nusach* ("melody") reserved for the three glorious concepts that form this important part of the Silent Devotion. Each of these sections is introduced with a historical narrative, followed by ten biblical verses: three from the Bible, three from the Writings, three from the Prophets and one last verse from the Bible. Following these verses is a final plea for G-d to be compassionate toward us as we are being judged. As the *Chazan* recites the concluding blessing of each section, the Congregation rises, in preparation for the blowing of the *shofar* which follows the blessing.

The order of the *shofar* blasts after each of the three groups is identical.

TEKIAH, SHEVARIM – TERUAH, TEKIAH,
TEKIAH, SHEVARIM, TEKIAH,
TEKIAH, TERUAH, TEKIAH.

At the conclusion of the third group we will have heard altogether sixty *shofar* blasts. [When *Rosh Hashanah* falls on *Shabbat,* the *shofar* is not sounded.]

Special hymns are recited during the *Chazan*'s repetition of the *Shemoneh Esray,* after each of the sections of *Malchuyot, Zichronot* and *Shofarot.*

HAYOM HARAT OLAM
("Today is the birthday of the world")

The hymn *Hayom Harat Olam is* recited after each section (i.e., once after *Malchuyot,* once after *Zichronot* and another time after *Shofarot*). We acknowledge in this hymn that this is the day that the world was created and we request that G-d judge us with mercy.

Chazan and Congregation sing together.

**Hayom harat olam, hayom ya-amid bamishpat,
kol yetzuray olamim, im k'vanim im ka-avadim.
Im k'vanim rachamaynu, k'rachaym av al banim;
v'im ka-avadim, aynaynu l'chah t'luyot.
Ad shet'chanaynu v'totzie kah-or mishpataynu
ayom kadosh.**

ARESHET S'FATAYNU
("May the words of our lips")

The second hymn recited is *Areshet S'fataynu* ("May the words of our lips"), a request to G-d to accept our *shofar* blasts together with all their profound meanings. [*If* Rosh Hashanah *falls on* Shabbat, Areshet S'fataynu *is not said.*]

Chazan *and Congregation sing together*

**Areshet s'fataynu, ye-erav l'fanechah, el ram v'nisah.
Mayvin u-ma-azin, mahbit umakshiv, l'kol tekiah-taynu.
Ut'kabayl b'rachamim uv'ratzon seder**
    Malchuyotaynu. *(Recited after the* Malchuyot *section).*
    Zichronotaynu. *(Recited after the* Zichronot *section).*
    Shofarotaynu. *(Recited after the* Shofarot *section).*

(For further explanation of the concepts of Malchuyot, Zichronot *and* Shofarot, *please see pages 59 and 61)*

At the conclusion of the last section, Shofarot, *the Congregation remains standing in preparation for the priestly blessing.*

☙ BIRKAT KOHANIM ❧
("The priestly blessing")

Day 1	A 522	BC 395	B 359	M 377	L 159
Day 2	A 572	BC 395	B 617	M 602	L 159

The priests hands are washed by the Levites present at the services. They then ascend to the *bimah* ("platform") in front of the *Aron*. After they remove their shoes, they prepare for the holy task assigned to them from the *Torah*. Through their raised hands will flow G-d's blessings for safety, sustenance and peace.

When the Temple still stood, the priests blessed the people every day of the year. Since the destruction of the Holy Temple in 70 C.E., in most synagogues outside of Israel, the priests bless the people only on holidays.

AVINU MALKAYNU, Z'CHOR
("Our Father, our King, remember")

Just prior to the priestly blessing, the Congregation and then the *Chazan* recite *Avinu Malkaynu*, asking G-d to remove sickness, evil and hatred from us.

Day 1 A 524 BC 397 B 361 M 379 L 159				
Day 2 A 572 BC 397 B 619 M 604 L 159				

Cong. recites, Chazan *repeats.*

**Avinu Malkaynu, z'chor rachamecha,
uch'vosh ka-as'cha, v'cha-lay dever,
v'che-rev, v'ra-av, ush'vi, umash-chit,
v'avon, u-magayfah, u-fegah ra,
v'chol machalah, v'chol takalah, v'chol k'tatah,
v'chol meenay fur-aniyot, v'chol g'zayrah ra-ah,
v'sinat chinam, may-alaynu,
u-may-al kol b'nay v'reetechah.**

U-CH'TOV
("And inscribe")

Immediately after *Avinu Malkaynu,* we say the third of the four special *Rosh Hashanah* phrases. It is recited prior to the blessing of *Hatov Shimcha* ("The Beneficent One").

Day 1 A 524 BC 397 B 361 M 379 L 159				
Day 2 A 574 BC 397 B 619 M 604 L 159				

Cong. recites, Chazan *repeats.*

Uch'tov l'chayim tovim kol b'nay v'ritecha.
("And inscribe all the children of your covenant for a good life.")

Y'VARECHEH-CHAH
("May He bless you")

While the *Kohanim* ("priests") bless us we avert our eyes so as not to distract them from giving us the blessings nor be distracted from receiving their blessing. At the recital of the last word of each of the following three blessings, the

Kohanim prolong the word by chanting a melody. This enables the Congregation to quietly recite a special supplication. [On the Sabbath, the final word is not prolonged.] The *Kohanim* now ask G-d to bless and safeguard us, to shine His face on us and be gracious to us and finally to grant us peace.

Day 1	A 526	BC 399	B 363	M 381	L 160
Day 2	A 576	BC 399	B 621	M 606	L 160

Chazan *recites each word,* Kohanim *repeat.*

Y'varecheh-chah, Adonai,
    v'Yish-me-rechah. *Cong. responds* Amen.
Ya-er, Adonai, Panav, Aylechah,
    Veey-chu-ne-kah. *Cong. responds* Amen.
Yisa, Adonai, Panav, Aylechah,
    v'Yasaym, L'chah, Shalom. *Cong. responds* Amen.

B'SEFER CHAYIM
("In the Book of Life")

This is the last of the special High Holiday phrases. The sentence is a final plea to G-d to remember us and the entire Jewish people and inscribe us for a good life and for peace, in the Book of Life.

Day 1	A 532	BC 405	B 369	M 387	L 161
Day 2	A 580	BC 405	B 627	M 612	L 161

Cong. *recites,* Chazan repeats.

B'sefer chayim b'racha v'shalom, ufarnasa tovah,
neezachayr v'neekatayv l'fanecha,
anachnu v'chol amcha bayt Yisrael,
l'chayim tovim ul'shalom.

V'NE-EMAR
("And may it be said")

In this prayer we declare our belief in the *Torah* and ask G-d to inscribe us in the Book of Life and accept our prayers. The Congregation joins the *Chazan* in a joyous melody in the second half. We ask that on this day (*Hayom*)

G-d strengthen us, bless us, hear our pleas, and accept our prayers.

Day 1	A 532	BC 405	B 369	M 387	L 161
Day 2	A 580	BC 405	B 627	M 612	L 161

Cong. recites, Chazan *repeats, or sung in unison.*

V'ne-emar, ki vi yirbu yamechah,
v'yosifu l'chah sh'not chayim.
L'chayim tovim tich-t'vaynu, Elohim chayim.
Katvaynu b'sefer hachayim, kakahtuv:
V'atem hadvaykim baAdonai Elohaychem,
chayim kulchem hayom.

THE *ARON* IS OPENED.

Chazan *recites each phrase,* Cong. *responds* Amen *and recites next phrase. In some Congregations,* Chazan *and* Cong. *sing the entire hymn.*

Hayom T'amtzaynu	**Amen.**
Hayom T'varchaynu	**Amen.**
Hayom T'gadlaynu	**Amen.**
Hayom Tidreshaynu l'tovah	**Amen.**
Hayom Tishma shava-taynu	**Amen.**
Hayom T'kabayl b'rachamim u'vratzon et t'filataynu	**Amen.**
Hayom Tit-m'chaynu biymin tzidkechah	**Amen.**

THE *ARON* IS CLOSED.

✍ KADDISH SHALAYM ✍
("Full *Kaddish*")

With a joyous melody, the *Chazan* recites the concluding part of the *Mussaf Shemoneh Esray*. With confidence we trust that our prayers will be accepted. Once again, the Congregation should respond with concentration and devotion, particularly, *Amen, Y'hay sh'may rabbah m'varach* . . . ("May His great name be blessed forever and ever").

Day 1	A 584	BC 407	B 371	M 389	L 162
Day 2	A 584	BC 407	B 629	M 614	L 162

Chazan *recites:*

Yitgadal, v'yitkadash, sh'may rabbah. *Cong. responds* Amen.

B'almah di-v'ra chirutay, v'yamlich malchutay, b'chayaychon uv'yomaychon, u'v'chayay d'chol bayt Yisrael, ba-agalah uvizman kareev, v'imru, Amen. *Cong. responds* Amen.

Chazan *and Cong.* recite *together:* **Y'hay sh'may rabbah m'varach, l'alam ul'almay almayah.**

Yitbarach, v'yishtabach, v'yit-pa-ar, v'yit-romam, v'yit-naseh, v'yit-hadar, v'yit-aleh, v'yit-halal, sh'may d'kudshah, B'rich Hu. *Cong. responds* B'rich Hu.

L'aylah, l'aylah, mikol birchatah v'shiratah, tush-b'chatah, v'ne-chematah, da-amiran b'almah, v'imru, Amen. *Cong. responds* Amen.

In many Congregations the Chazan *halts now for the blowing of another thirty* shofar *blasts. Please see page 54 for the order of the* shofar *sounds. (We have now listened to ninety* shofar *blasts altogether.) [The* shofar *is not sounded when* Rosh Hashanah *occurs on the Sabbath.]*

Titkabel tz'lot-hon u-va-ut-hon d'chol bayt Yisrael, kadam avu-hon di vish-maya, v'imru, Amen. *Cong. responds* Amen.

Y'hay sh'lama rabbah min sh'maya, v'chayim, alaynu v'al kol Yisrael, v'imru, Amen. *Cong. responds* Amen.

Oseh hashalom bimro-mav, Hu ya-aseh shalom, alaynu v'al kol Yisrael, v'imru, Amen. *Cong. responds* Amen.

℣ CONCLUDING HYMNS ℞

At the conclusion of the service we express our joy through song. This reflects our confidence in G-d that He has accepted our prayers.

AYN KAYLOHAYNU
("There is none like our G-d")

Day 1 A 586	BC 409	B 373	M 391	L 162
Day 2 A 586	BC 409	B 631	M 615	L 162

Ayn Kaylohaynu,   Ayn KaAdonaynu,

Ayn K'malkaynu,   Ayn K'moshiaynu.

Mi Chaylohaynu,   Mi ChaAdonaynu,
Mi Ch'malkaynu,   Mi Ch'moshiaynu.

Nodeh Laylohaynu, Nodeh LaAdonaynu,
Nodeh L'malkaynu, Nodeh L'moshiaynu.

Baruch Elohaynu,   Baruch Adonaynu,
Baruch Malkaynu,   Baruch Moshiaynu.

Ata hu Elohaynu,   Ata hu Adonaynu,
Ata hu Malkaynu,   Ata hu Moshiaynu.

Ata hu sheh-hiktiru, avotaynu,
L'fanecha, et ketoret hasamim.

ALAYNU

("It is our duty")

For the last 700 years this has been the final prayer of each of the daily prayers, and each of the Festival and Sabbath prayers. In the 9th century Rabbi Hai Ben David Gaon wrote that this sublime prayer was composed by Joshua as he brought the Jews into the promised land. Throughout the centuries, *Alaynu* was prohibited or censored in many countries.

Day 1	A 590	BC 415	B 379	M 396	L 164
Day 2	A 590	BC 415	B 637	M 621	L 164

Alaynu l'shabayach la-adon hakol,
latayt g'dula l'yotzayr b'raysheet.
Shelo asanu k'goyay ha-aratzot,
v'lo samanu k'mishp'chot ha-adama.
Sheh-lo sam chelkaynu kahem,
v'goralaynu k'chol hamonam.

(Chazan *and Congregation bow at the underlined words*)
Va-anachnu kor'im umishtachavim umodim,
lifnay melech malchay ham'lachim,
Hakadosh Baruch Hu.
Shehu noteh shamayim v'yosed aretz,

umoshav y'karo bashamayim mima-al,
u'shchinat uzo b'govhay m'romim.
Hu Elohaynu, ayn od.
Emet malkaynu, efes zulato,
ka-katuv b'torato, v'yadata hayom va-hashay-vota
el l'vavecha, ki Adonai hu ha-Elohim
bashamayim mima-al, v'al ha-aretz mitachat ayn od.

The final verse:

V'ne-emar, v'haya Adonai l'melech al kol ha-aretz,
bayom ha-hu yihyeh Adonai echad ush'mo echad.

✂ KADDISH YATOM ✂
("Mourner's *Kaddish*")

The *Mourner's Kaddish* is recited for eleven months following the death of a parent at every Congregational Service. It is also recited on the anniversary *(Yahrtzeit)* of the death. *Kaddish* is a source of merit for the soul and the most important part is the Congregational response, *Amen, Y'hay sh'may rabbah m'varach . . .*

Day 1	A 592	BC 417	B 381	M 398	L 174
Day 2	A 592	BC 417	B 639	M 623	L 174

Mourner recites:

Yitgadal, v'yitkadash, sh'may rabbah. *Cong. responds* Amen.
B'almah di-v'ra chirutay, v'yamlich malchutay,
b'chayaychon uv'yomaychon, u'v'chayay d'chol
bayt Yisrael, ba-agalah uvizman kareev,
v'imru, **Amen.** *Cong. responds* Amen.

Chazan and Cong. recite together: Y'hay sh'may rabbah m'varach,
l'alam ul'almay almayah.

Yitbarach, v'yishtabach, v'vit-pa-ar, v'yit-romam,
v'yit-naseh, v'yit-hadar, v'yit-aleh, v'yit-halal,
sh'may d'kudshah, B'rich Hu. *Cong. responds* B'rich Hu.

L'aylah, l'aylah, mikol birchatah v'shiratah,
tushb'chatah, v'ne-chematah, da-amiran b'almah,

v'imru, Amen. *Cong. responds* Amen.

Y'hay shlamah rabbah min sh'mayah, v'chayim,
alaynu v'al kol Yisrael, v'imru, Amen. *Cong. responds* Amen.

Oseh hashalom bimromav, hu ya-aseh shalom,
alaynu v'al kol Yisrael, v'imru, Amen. *Cong. responds* Amen.

Following the daily Psalm, ten additional *shofar* blasts are sounded to complete the necessary one hundred *shofar* blasts. [The *shofar* is not sounded when *Rosh Hashanah* falls on the Sabbath.]

TEKIAH, SHEVARIM – TERUAH, TEKIAH,
TEKIAH, SHEVARIM, TEKIAH,
TEKIAH, TERUAH, TEKIAH G'DOLAH.

L'DAVID ADONAI ORI V'YISHEE
("Of David, G-d is my light and salvation")

Day 1 A 178	BC 417	B 381	M 405	L 113
Day 2 A 178	BC 417	B 639	M 631	L 113

Psalm 27, *L'David Adonai Ori V'yishee* is now recited. This Psalm is especially appropriate for the High Holidays and contains allusions to the entire penitential period. If there are mourners in the synagogue the *Kaddish Yatom* follows.

ADON OLAM
("Eternal Lord")

This hymn expresses our absolute trust in G-d's omnipotence and permanence. While *Olam* can mean both eternity and world, here it is generally understood to refer to the eternity of the Lord.

Adon Olam has been attributed to various medieval poets, and was most likely written by the Spanish poet Solomon Ibn Gabriol in the 11th century, although it may date back to Babylonian times.

Day 1	A 180	BC 419	B 383	M 636	L 49
Day 2	A 180	BC 419	B 643	M 636	L 49

Adon olam asher malach, b'terem kol y'tzir nivrah,
L'ayt na-a-sa b'cheftzo kol, ahzay melech sh'mo nikrah.

V'acharay kichlot ha-kol, l'vado yimloch norah,
V'hu haya v'hu hoveh, v'hu yihyeh b'tifarah.

V'hu echad, v'ayn shaynee, l'hamsheel lo l'hachbirah,
B'li raysheet, b'li tachlit, v'lo ha-ohz v'hamisrah.

V'hu ayli, v'chai go-ali, v'tzur chevli b'ayt tzarah,
V'hu neesi u-manos li, m'nat kosi b'yom ekrah.

B'yado afkid ruchi, b'ayt eeshan v'ah-eerah,
V'im ruchi g'viyati, Adonai li v'lo eerah.

One leaves the synagogue content and filled with confidence that our prayers will be accepted. We greet each other with blessings for the New Year, or simply say *Good Yom Tov* ("Happy Holiday"). Upon arrival at home, we recite the *Kiddush* and enjoy a festive meal.

In the afternoon . . .

It is ideal to spend the balance of the day reading from the Psalms or other holy books and meditating on what the New Year means to us.

It is customary on the afternoon of *Rosh Hashanah* to recite the prayer of *Tashlich.* This prayer symbolizes our hope that G-d will forgive our sins on the Days of Awe. We go to a body of water to recite *Tashlich.* This impresses upon us that just as the body is purified by water, so can our souls be purified by repentance. If one is unable to recite the prayer on either of the two days, it may be said at any time during the Penitential period.

☙ The Broken Heart ❧

he renowned 18th century founder of Chasidism, the Baal Shem Tov, was preparing for *Rosh Hashanah*. He chose Rabbi Zev Kitzes to call out the names of the *shofar* sounds and asked him to spend time learning the secret meanings of the *shofar* blasts. Rabbi Kitzes spent a long time learning, and in order to remember the secret meanings he wrote them down on a little slip of paper.

Rosh Hashanah arrived and when it was time for the Baal Shem Tov to blow the *shofar*, Rabbi Kitzes, thinking that he had put the secret codes in his *kittel* (white shroud-like coat), began looking for the slip of paper. He couldn't find it anywhere *and* he couldn't remember the special meanings of the *shofar* sounds. Broken hearted and contrite he called out the *shofar* sounds in a weeping voice.

When the Baal Shem Tov completed the *shofar* blowing, he went to Rabbi Zev and congratulated him for learning the most important meaning of the *shofar*. He told Rabbi Zev that the different sounds of the *shofar* and their secret meanings are the keys to opening the gates in heaven. Of all the keys, though, only one key can open *all* the gates—a broken heart. When someone sincerely expresses their most profound feelings before G-d, their prayers can enter through all the gates of Heaven.

Turning the Scale

In the *Talmud* it is written "Because the world is judged by its majority and an individual too is judged by their majority of deeds—good or bad—if one good deed is performed, happy is the person for turning the scale both for themselves and for the whole world on the side of merit." (*Kiddushin* 40a).

Mincha
The Afternoon Service

A 598 BC 425 B 389 M 409 L 186

he introductory prayers for the *Mincha Service* are *Ashray* and *Uvah L'tziyon,* and they are recited by the Congregation and the *Chazan.* When the first day of *Rosh Hashanah* falls on a weekday, the Half *Kaddish* is recited. *(Please see following page.)* When *Rosh Hashanah's* first day falls on *Shabbat,* we publicly read the first portion of the following week's Bible portion. Only one *Torah* Scroll is used for the *Mincha* Service.

The *Torah* Reading is from *Deuteronomy* 32:1-12, the Portion *(parsha)* of *Ha-azeenu.* Three men, a *Kohayn,* a *Levi* and a *Yisrael,* are called to recite blessings. *(Please refer to The Torah Service, page 47, for transliterations.)*

A 608 BC 435 B 399 M 429 L 189

After the reading, the *Torah* is lifted and the Congregation chants *V'zot Hatorah. (See page 48 for transliteration.)*

The *Torah* Scroll is then returned to the *Aron* and the hymns accompanying the return of the *Torah* are recited. *(Please see page 55 for transliteration.)*

❧ HALF KADDISH ❧

A 602 BC 439 B 403 M 424 L 199

In this beautiful and ancient prayer we ask that G-d's name be exalted in the world. The most important part is the Congregational response, *Amen, Y'hay sh'may rabbah m'varach* . . . ("May His great name be blessed forever and ever"), which should be fervently recited aloud. *(Please see page 58 for transliteration.)*

❧ SHEMONEH ESRAY ❧
(Silent Devotion)

A 612 BC 439 B 403 M 424 L 190

See your *Machzor* for the *Shemonah Esray*. The *Shemoneh Esray* should be recited softly. Many people gently rock during prayer as an aid to concentration. *(Please refer to pages 9 and 60 for an in-depth explanation.)*

❧ CHAZARAT HASHATZ ❧
("*Chazan*'s Repetition")

As in all the other services, the *Chazan*'s repetition is communal prayer, and several of the most important parts of the service are included in the repetition. At various points, the *Aron* is opened and the Congregation rises.

Some of the more significant prayers:

❧ KEDUSHAH ❧

A 614 BC 441 B 405 M 426 L 191

("Sanctification of G-d's Name")

The Children of Israel join with the angels in praising G-d in the *Kedushah*.

Cong. and Chazan *together.*

N'kadaysh et shimchah ba-olam,
k'shaym sheh-makdishim oto, bishmay marom,
kakatoov al yad n'vee-echa,
v'karah zeh el zeh v'amar.

Cong. and Chazan *together. During the words* Kadosh, Kadosh, Kadosh, *we rise on our toes.*

Kadosh, Kadosh, Kadosh, Adonai Tz'va-ot,
Meloh Chal Ha-aretz K'vodo.

Cong. recites, Chazan *repeats.*

L'umatam baruch yomayru.

Cong. and Chazan *together. During the word* Baruch *we rise on our toes.*

Baruch K'vod Adonai Mimkomo.

Cong. recites, Chazan *repeats.*

Uv'divray kadsh'cha katoov laymor.

Cong. and Chazan *together. During the word* Yimloch *we rise on our toes.*

Yimloch Adonai L'olam, Elohayich Tziyon,
L'dor Vador, Halleluyah.

❧ AVINU MALKAYNU ☙
("Our Father, our King")

A 622 BC 449 B 413 M 437 L195

At the conclusion of the *Chazan*'s repetition of the Silent Devotion we recite the *Avinu Malkaynu*, a series of 44 verses of supplication. Nine verses particularly pertinent to the High Holidays are recited by the *Chazan* and repeated by the Congregation. In many Congregations the last verse is sung together. [*Avinu Malkaynu* is not recited on the Sabbath.]

THE *ARON* IS OPENED.

*The following is an excerpt from
the 15th to the 24th line of* Avinu Malkaynu.

Chazan *recites each line, Cong. repeats.*

Avinu Malkaynu, hacha-zee-raynu bit'shuvah
sh'laymah l'fanecha.

Avinu Malkaynu, sh'lach r'fuah sh'laymah l'cholay amecha.
Avinu Malkaynu, k'ra ro-ah g'zar deenaynu.
Avinu Malkaynu, zachraynu b'zeekaron tov l'fanecha.
Avinu Malkaynu, katvaynu b'sefer chayim tovim.
Avinu Malkaynu, katvaynu b'sefer g'ulah vee'shuah.
Avinu Malkaynu, katvaynu b'sefer parnasah v'chalkalah.
Avinu Malkaynu, katvaynu b'sefer z'chuyot.
Avinu Malkaynu, katvaynu b'sefer s'lichah um'cheelah.

Last verse:

Avinu Malkaynu, chanaynu va-anaynu
 ki ayn banu ma-asim.
Aseh imanu, tz'dakah va-chesed, v'hoshiaynu.

THE *ARON* IS CLOSED.

✍ KADDISH SHALAYM ✶
("Full *Kaddish*")

A 626 BC 453 B 417 M 441 L 197

The final part of the service is the *Full Kaddish*, wherein G-d's name is extolled and we pray that our service will be accepted. *(Please refer to page 80 for transliteration.)*

ALAYNU
("It is our duty")

A 626 BC 455 B 419 M 442 L 198

For the last 700 years this has been the final prayer of each of the daily prayers, and each of the Festival and Sabbath prayers. In the 9th century Rabbi Hai Ben David Gaon wrote that this sublime prayer was composed by Joshua as he brought the Jews into the promised land. Throughout the centuries, *Alaynu* was prohibited or censored in many countries. *(Please see page 82 for transliteration.)*

If there are mourners in the synagogue, the Kaddish Yatom, *the Mourner's* Kaddish, *would follow* Alaynu. *(Please see page 83 for transliteration.)*

Maariv
(Concluding Service)

A 646 BC — B — M — L 202

Rosh Hashanah ends with the recital of the weekday Evening Service and the *Havdalah*. See your *Machzor* or *Siddur (Prayer Book)* for these Services.

May we all be written and inscribed for a happy, healthy and sweet New Year. May we speedily see the redemption of our people and the coming of the Messiah, and may all our prayers be answered. Let us finally see a true peace for us and our beloved State of Israel and may we be privileged to be in Jerusalem this coming year to witness the rebuilding of our Temple, *Bimhayrah V'yamaynu,* ("speedily and in our day"), Amen.

FIFTEEN YEAR CALENDAR
ROSH HASHANA (FIRST DAY)

1994	5755	Tuesday	September 6
1995	5756	Monday	September 25
1996	5757	Saturday	September 14
1997	5758	Thursday	October 2
1998	5759	Monday	September 21
1999	5760	Saturday	September 11
2000	5761	Saturday	September 30
2001	5762	Tuesday	September 18
2002	5763	Saturday	September 7
2003	5764	Saturday	September 27
2004	5765	Thursday	September 16
2005	5766	Tuesday	October 4
2006	5767	Saturday	September 23
2007	5768	Thursday	September 13
2008	5769	Tuesday	September 30

❧ GLOSSARY ☙

Aliyah. "Ascent." As used in the synagogue, it refers to being called up to the *bimah* to recite the Blessings of the *Torah*.

Amen. "It is true." Also an acronym for *El Melech Ne-eman*, "G-d is a faithful King." It is the response recited after a blessing, and indicates belief in the words of the blessing.

Amidah. "Standing." The silent devotional prayer recited while standing. It is the most essential part of the prayer service. Also called *Shemoneh Esray.*

Amud. "Pillar." In the synagogue, it refers to the stand from which the *Chazan* leads the congregation.

Aron Kodesh. "Holy Ark." Always located at the front of the synagogue, usually facing Jerusalem, it houses the *Torah* scrolls.

Avodah. "Service." Historically, the term referred to the sacrificial service in the Holy Temple. Since the destruction of the Temple, the term is used to refer to the prayer service, which took the place of the sacrificial service.

Ba-al Koreh. "Master of reading." A person trained in the intricacies of reading from the *Torah* scroll without cantillation and punctuation marks.

Ba-al Tefilah. "Master of prayer." See *Chazan.*

Bimah. "Platform." The platform in the synagogue from which the *Torah* scroll is read.

Birkat Hamazon. Grace after meals.

Brachah. "Blessing." A sanctification of G-d's Name, which takes the form of thanks or praise. One who hears a *Brachah* recited is obligated to answer "*Amen.*"

Chazan. "Cantor." One who leads the congregation in prayer.

Haftarah. "To dismiss" or "to complete." The section of the Prophets, publicly read, that corresponds with the Bible portion.

Hallel. "Praise." A collections of Psalms of Praise recited on Festivals.

Havdalah. "Separation." Ceremony performed at the conclusion of *Shabbat* which proclaims the division between *Shabbat* and the ensuing days of the week.

Hoshanah Rabbah. Literally, "The Great *Hoshanah* ('please save.')". Actually it is the name of the last of the Intermediary days *(Chol Ha Moed)* of *Sukkot*. It is also the final day that the Four Species can be used.

Kaddish. "Sanctification." An ancient prayer, mostly in Aramaic, sanctifying G-d's Name. Of the several types of *Kaddish*, one is recited by mourners as a benefit for the soul of the departed.

Kittel. White outer garment customarily worn on specific religious occasions, such as *Yom Kippur*. Also worn as a burial shroud.

Kohayn pl. **Kohanim.** "Priest." A descendant of Aaron, brother of Moses. The *Kohanim* were responsible to perform the sacrificial service in the Holy Temple. In our times, the *Kohanim* still act as G-d's servants by performing the priestly blessing over the congregation.

Kohayn Gadol. "High Priest." When the Holy Temple stood, the *Kohayn Gadol* performed many of the most important functions, such as the *Yom Kippur* service.

Levi. A descendant of the tribe of Levi, (Jacob's third son). The Levites served as gatekeepers and musicians in the Holy Temple.

Maariv. Literally, "brings on [evening]" or "moves [the sun] to the West." The evening prayer.

Machzor. Literally, "cycle." The festival prayerbook.

Maftir. Literally, "conclusion." The person who receives the concluding *Aliyah* of the *Torah* reading, and who afterwards reads the *Haftarah*.

Mezuzah. Literally, "doorpost." A small scroll containing certain portions of the *Torah*, written according to exacting specifications and affixed to the doorpost of every doorway leading into a living area.

Midrash. Compilation of Rabbinic lore, including

anecdotal, moral and philosphical expositions on the *Torah*.

Mincha. Literally, "meal-offering." The afternoon prayer service, which replaced the afternoon offering in the Holy Temple.

Mishnah. The codification of the Oral Law, as set down in 63 tractates by Rabbi Judah the Prince around 200 C.E.

Mitzvah, pl. **mitzvot.** "Commandment." The *Torah* prescribes 613 *mitzvot*, requiring us to either take or refrain from a certain action.

Mussaf. "Additional." The additional prayer recited on *Shabbat* and festivals, corresponding to the additional offering that was brought to the Holy Temple on these special days.

Parsha. "Division." A section of the *Torah* consisting of at least three verses.

Piyut, pl. **piyutim.** Liturgical poems, most of which originated in the early centuries of the Common Era and in the Middle Ages.

Sedrah. pl. **Sedrot.** "[Part of a] series." The portion of the *Torah* read on *Shabbat* in the synagogue.

Selichot. "Forgiveness." Penitential prayers recited during the New Year season and on fast days, expressing remorse for our sins.

Shacharit. "Morning." The morning prayers.

Shemoneh Esray. See *Amidah*.

Shofar. The ram's horn upon which a series of blasts is sounded on *Rosh Hashanah*; one blast is also sounded at the conclusion of the *N'eelah* service of *Yom Kippur*.

Simchat Torah. "The rejoicing over the *Torah*." The holiday immediately following *Succot* on which we celebrate the completion of the annual *Torah* reading cycle.

Succah. pl. **Succot.** "Booth" or "tabernacle." A temporary residence built for the festival of *Succot*.

Tallit pl. **tallitot.** "Garment." As used in the synagogue, it refers to the prayer shawl worn by men during the prayer service.

Talmud. "Teaching." The oral explanation and discussion of the *Mishnah*, committed to writing and codified by Rav Ami and Rav Assi, heads of the Babylonian teaching academies, in the fifth century C.E.

Tashlich. Literally, "Throw away or cast away." The word comes from a verse in the book of *Micah* which describes how G-d will cast away our sins. *Tashlich* refers to the custom of going to a body of water on *Rosh Hashanah* to recite a collection of prayers through which we can symbolically rid ourselves of our sins.

Tefillin. "Phylacteries." Small black leather boxes which contain certain Biblical passages, worn upon the arm and head of Jewish males over the age of thirteen.

Teshuvah. "Return." The term used for repentance for past sins. True *teshuvah* requires an admission of guilt as well as a firm resolve never to repeat the sin.

Tishray. The seventh month of the Jewish year.

Torah. "Teaching." Strictly speaking, this term refers only to the Five Books of Moses. However, all knowledge and teaching deriving from G-d's Revelation at Sinai is collectively known as *Torah*.

Tzitzit. "Fringes." The *Torah* commands a Jewish male to attach fringes to any four-cornered garment, so that by seeing them, he will be reminded of G-d's commandments.

Yahrzeit. "Year time." This is a Yiddish term used to refer to the anniversary of a death.